The Mighty Bluefin

The Mighty Bluefin

A 50-year fishery of the fisherman's fiercest fighting fish

By Capt. Roger Jarvis,
also author of **The Bottom Dunker's bible — how to find and fish for the finest finny food**

Jones River Press

Plymouth, Mass. • 2005

Editing and design: Doris M. Johnson, Jones River Press,
Box 6039, Plymouth, MA 02362
800-498-3899 • www.jones-river-press.com

Also by Roger Jarvis: The Bottom Dunker's Bible — how to find and fish for the finest finny food

Cataloging-in-Publication Data
Jarvis, Roger, author

Bluefin —

22 photographs
224 pages, including acknowledgement, foreword and introduction

1. Sports; fishing

I. Title II. Atlantic coast III. Fish species IV. Roger Jarvis (author)

ISBN 1-888964-18-9 paperback
ISBN 1-888964-19-7 casebound

Printed in the United States of America

Acknowledgements

First and foremost, I must acknowledge the advice and editing received from my mate, companion, friend and partner, all in the person of my wife, Sandra! Her help and advice in the day-to-day production of this book has been invaluable.

Secondly, I am indebted to Doris Johnson for her editing and publishing expertise as owner of the Jones River Press of Plymouth, Mass.

Thinking of those who taught me the most about the tuna fishery, I must start with the three "Giants" covered in Part II. Manny Philips, Joe Eldridge and Donald Hebert are the three fishermen from whom I gained the most. They were each the type of person who taught by example. You only needed to watch and listen — using open eyes and ears and a mind like a sponge — to gain a volume of expert advice to apply to your day-to-day work on the water.

I must mention one more fisherman who has become a mentor of my life's passion. Charley Soares is an outdoor writer, a teacher, charter captain and a superb seminar speaker. We have worked together and fished together for the last quarter of a century. He is my mentor, but most important, I am privileged to have him as a friend.

There is no way I could list the hundreds of other men and women from which I have gained knowledge of the sea and its creatures. The experienced members of the fishing fraternity are gracious and giving, and I have been very fortunate to meet and share ideas and experiences with many of them.

There are two organizations with which I have been involved since 1970: Cape Cod Charter Boat Association & Green Harbor (Mass.) Tuna Club. I'm honored to have been one of the founders of the GHTC, as well as having been elected president of both it and the CCCBA. These two organizations have had a preponderance of dedicated and knowledgeable fishermen throughout their existence. I have had many "give and take" sessions with their members and my hope is that I have helped them as much as I have learned from them.

And finally — to all those involved in the bluefin fishery — safe passage, calm seas, and again . . . . . tight lines and sharp hooks!

— Capt. Roger Jarvis

About This Book

I first decided to write about the mighty bluefin as the 20th century was coming to a close, and I realized I had 30 years of experience in the fishery. I did some research and found that both recreational & commercial fishermen first targeted the bluefin around the mid-1950s. This meant I had entered the fishery early, only 15 years after it began. (see Chapter 2 - A Brief History.)

Checking my ship's logs for that period, doing a little math showed that I had spent the equivalent of two full years of my life on Stellwagen Bank - the majority of that time spent chartering and commercial fishing in the tuna fishery.

I must confess that my respect for this formidable adversary grew with each one I bested; so much so that I always felt a pang of remorse for having killed such a magnificent creature. This respect is responsible for my views on the necessity to insure the preservation of this species for generations to come. The ideal situation, of course, would be a healthy and sustainable fishery large enough to afford access to all the user groups.

Besides looking back on how the fishery developed, I have included what I have found to be the average fisherman's feelings about the way government bureaus (federal, state, and sometimes even local governments) regulate and complicate their control over the fishery. Some regulations seem to deliberately pit the various user groups against each other with allocation, quotas, geographic areas, and seasonal closings - confusing and exasperating to all permit holders.

Each chapter includes information that is the result of interviews, research, or personal experiences having to do with the observation or capture of the strongest and most evolved member of the bony fishes.

Special note: chapters with their title in italics are those in which this author has injected a little of his own "poetic license." They are based on actual happenings, either personally experienced or observed, but the names of the individuals involved have been changed to protect the guilty. So many things can go wrong when trying to best this powerful animal that the guilty need all the protection they can get!

I have used the real names of the participants in the rest of the chapters, and have stuck closely to the truth of the events as they happened.

I wish the readers a bountiful catch whenever they engage in their piscatorial pursuits. May the fishing gods always give you safe passage to your home port.

Tight lines and sharp hooks —
Capt. Roger Jarvis

Introduction

This book stinks of sun-ripened chum, cold coffee, and musty high school auditoriums where fisheries policy takes shape. It shouts like the sound of a screaming drag, a diesel engine in full reverse, and creaking fighting-chair gimbals. It puts readers face-to-face with the diverse characters that have abandoned gainful employment for the manic-depressive lifestyle that belongs to the bluefin tuna fleet.

Giant tackle, giant expenses, giant fish and giant paychecks. Add to those: giant tempers, giant time expenditures, giant victories and giant losses. Bluefin fishing is, well, giant in scale. It's no wonder this fishery attracts fanatics of a degree unmatched by any other angling discipline! (I challenge you to name a surf-fisherman who'd trade his house, car, job and marriage for an undersized vessel and fishing gear so he could attempt to land a fish that could easily kill him.)

From a writing standpoint, the bluefin is a giant topic, one that has inspired countless scientific papers, essays, short stories, novels, non-fiction books and feature articles. What has been missing, thus far, is a book written from firsthand experience that paints the whole picture. Captain Roger Jarvis's love/hate affair with giant bluefin tuna is giving us just that, all the while maintaining his sense of humor, wonderment, humility, authority and clarity.

The old adage that the "sum is greater than the total of its parts" should guide you through these pages. In here, a man who has fished for bluefin for 30 years begins at the beginning and includes every important and diverse detail. This is not a blow-by-blow history of bluefin, a biological study, a fish tale, a management plan or a detailed outline of "how to" catch bluefin. It is all of these and then some.

In these pages, you'll laugh at the futility as you chafe under a scorching sun on your 16th straight fishless day. You'll revel in the victory as a cockpit harpoon buttonholes a fish that outweighs the family car. You'll flash with anger as you watch fishery managers allow an important species to be pushed to the brink of extinction. And you'll watch otherwise rational humans descend into the death rattles of tuna fever. In short, whether you are an old hand on deck or a rank amateur, you'll run the gamut of the bluefin fishing discipline.

It's all here for the reading, and if you've ever even wondered about bluefin tuna, you owe yourself a few hours by the fireplace with Bluefin.

Zach Harvey

— Editor, *NewEngland Fisherman*

Bluefin - *Table Of Contents*

Jeff and Doug Amorello, both of whom worked as mates on Capt Jarvis's charters, were happy to snag this 956-pounder themselves.

Part I – Getting to Know You

Chapter 1 -

The Mighty Bluefin - Like No Other

The CEO of a major Chicago corporation called me on a Monday in mid-July of 1976, asking if my charter boat, *Misty*, was available for the next two days. I glanced at my schedule, said it was not, but added that it was open on both Thursday and Friday. Without hesitation, he said he would fly into Logan Airport on Wednesday evening and meet me at 0600, Thursday morning. I gave him the directions to Green Harbor in Marshfield, Mass., and told him that *Misty* was berthed at the gas dock of the marina.

Thursday morning on the way to the tuna grounds, John (the CEO) told me that he had caught both blue and white marlin in the Caribbean, a great white shark on Australia's Great Barrier Reef, halibut off Alaska, a sailfish from the surf in Cozumel on the Yucatan Peninsula, etc., etc. In short, the man had "been there, done that" on most of the world's best fishing grounds.

The one specie he said he had never hooked into was a bluefin tuna. He said he had heard that they were like no other creature in the sea and he wanted to experience the feel of a giant bluefin.

Bruce, my mate, was a bit skeptical about all the exploits John was claiming, and I had to admit that they did seem a bit exaggerated. Yet for some reason, I had the feeling this passenger had it all together and was not a prevaricating about his piscatorial exploits.

The water was flat-ass-calm. With no breeze stirring, the air was hot and close as soon as *Misty* fetched up on its anchor in the tuna grounds. Bruce began to "chop and plop," setting up a strong slick. As the strength of the current changed, he adjusted the depth of the baits to keep them in the slick.

John and I were seated on the bridge, facing aft. I was scanning the other boats of the fleet to see if anyone was hooked up, while John watched Bruce working the cockpit. John mentioned how good Bruce was and how important a really good mate is. I concurred and told John that Bruce had been with me for over two years, and was the best mate I'd ever had. I knew how lucky I was to have him aboard.

As I watched John, I noticed that nothing within range of our seeing and hearing was getting past him. John had obviously spent enough time at sea to qualify as a seaman. I knew, if we hooked up, we would soon find out if he was also an angler!

The fleet was typical for a Thursday in mid-July, about 55 or 60 boats, and they were all doing their chum-thing with as much enthusiasm as one could expect from crews coping with a hot, windless day. By mid-afternoon, there had been only one hook-up and that ended with a spit-back hook before the boat had cleared the fleet.

Bruce looked over and gave me his head-for-the-barn shrug as the last few chunks of chum sank from sight. I told John we still had tomorrow, as I keyed the ignition and Bruce went forward to set up the anchor retrieval system. *(See Chapter 24: Special Gear & Tactics)*

John and I spent the lazy ride back to Green Harbor on the

The profile of a bluefin

bridge with Bruce in the tuna tower scanning for any activity that might disturb the glassy surface and lead to a chance to stick a fish. (Bruce has great eyes and is one of the best with a harpoon!)

Our conversation was entirely centered on bluefin tuna with John serving as the asker and me as the askee. Here was a middle-aged man with the enthusiasm and inquisitiveness of a young teen. I began to look forward to spending another day with this gentleman.

The next morning had a very memorable beginning. I always plan to be aboard at least 15 minutes prior to departure time, so I can have everything ready for the charter. As I swung my leg over the gunwale, at 0540, I was greeted with a hearty, "Good morning, Captain" from the bridge. John smiled and wanted to know why I was only 20 minutes early, and would I like a cup of coffee? This was starting out to be a good day!

Bruce arrived, as usual, just before 0600 with his 24 oz mug of Pepsi, said "Hi, Cap" to me and "Good morning" to John, and busied himself casting off the dock lines and stowing the gear.

We rounded the East jetty and I brought *Misty* to 090°. John sniffed the freshening breeze, smiled and said, "I hope this weather change means there will be more activity on the grounds today." I replied that a breeze after a flat-ass-calm day usually makes for a better bite, but these fish are smart and they always determine when, where and what they will eat. A good tuna fisherman is always honing his skills but ultimately, he has to go with the flow or he'll become a bundle of frustration and wind up as a drunk, a blithering idiot, or even worse. (Tuna fishing may be one of the causes of an increased divorce rate in New England – *see p. 179, Chapter 21.*)

On our way to the SW corner of Stellwagen Bank, Bruce cut up two buckets of chum and made one bucket of "chum soup" so we could be ready to start a strong slick as soon as *Misty* was anchored.

Two miles from the Bank, we could see several boats on anchor with their bows pointed into the breeze and two more boats approaching on our starboard side. The boat that really drew our attention was the one about a half-mile dead ahead with his stern into the chop. John pointed and asked if I thought that guy was hooked-up. "He isn't underway and boats don't drift into the current," I replied as I slowed speed and brought *Misty* to a course that would give the boat plenty of room to work the fish. It was only 0640 and already there had been at least this one hook-up. This had the potential to be a very good day.

There was no room between the anchored boats along the drop off on either side of the notch, so I maintained my course to the SE. I reasoned that the Northerly breeze might have caused the fish to move more to the South'ard to take advantage of the sand eels being swept over the edge of the very steep south drop-off by the breeze.

Bruce went forward to handle the anchor just before I turned into the wind and stopped *Misty's* momentum. He glanced to starboard and then to port, noticed we were away from the growing fleet, and shot me another sign of approval.

When we had fetched tight to the anchor, John and I descended to the cockpit to help set out the gear. John broadcast a ladle of "soup" and threw several pieces of chum to both starboard and port to get a slick started. I deployed the rig for the port rod and then placed the rod in its holder.

Bruce had finished with the starboard rod and was dropping back the balloon for the center rig when the rod I had deployed arched over as the line began to sing off the reel! Bruce yelled, "We're on!" He handed John the center rod and ordered him to, "clear it, then clear the starboard rod, stow them below, and then get back and into the bucket harness on the chair… on-the-double!" He said all this as he grabbed the port rod and set the hook with authority. (Bruce had never been in the service, but he sure would make a great drill sergeant.)

I bounded up the ladder to the bridge, started the engine, and pulled the quick release to our anchor ball. There was no need to back down; the fish already had *Misty* making sternway. I looked down at the cockpit where John, seated in the fighting chair, was holding the rod in the gimbal, while Bruce was snapping the bucket harness to the reel. The rod had a pronounced curve and the spool was still slowly backing off line. I could feel the boat gradually accelerating.

John was leaning back into the fighting chair with arms extended, but slightly bent at the elbows, in the classic stance of an expert angler. I asked him if he was ready to go to work. John nodded his head in the affirmative and held on. Bruce looked up, winked, and gave his OK sign of approval. *Misty* and her crew had passed the first major hurdle of a good tuna day — the hook-up.

"OK, from now on, I'll make all the decisions, but you and the mate will have to keep me informed as to any changes in the fish's movements. As of now, we are a three-man team that has to WANT that giant more than anything. Let's concentrate and keep in sync. For now, we'll stay in the towing mode." As I made this declaration, Bruce added just enough drag to prevent the spool from paying out line.

The spool was half empty so we knew the quarry was about 300 yards away. (Imagining the length of three football fields is a good way to get a mental visual picture.) I took a quick glance at the water surrounding *Misty*. There were no boats within two miles and the fish was towing us, stern first, directly toward the Provincetown Monument, some 11 miles to the South'ard.

Six or seven minutes had passed, with the tuna towing us at an estimated 2 or 3 knots, when suddenly the rod straightened. Bruce called out, "He's turned and is charging the boat. Crank that reel like a bastard John!" John was already spinning the handle like a pro.

I slipped into gear and made a 90° turn to port to produce a bow in the line while Bruce backed off the drag a little. (These last two actions put some forgiveness in the line to prevent snapping when the line become taut again.) So far, we were all on the same page.

When the curve in the rod began to straighten, I made another turn, this time to starboard, so both the fish and *Misty* would be on a parallel course back toward the fleet. Bruce had turned the chair to the starboard quarter and told John to be ready for the line to tighten. Bruce reported that John had gained about 100 yards.

The line tightened and once again line was being pulled from the spool; this time by the pressure generated by the line itself dragging through the water. This time John set the drag himself. Bruce looked up and gave me another OK sign.

The fish was swimming on the same course I was steering, about two football fields off our starboard side. I leaned over the aft bridge railing and said, "Let's see how long this guy will stay in this parallel mode. We have a chance to work him hard now. John, if he gives at all, gain what you can and keep the pressure on him."

Each time I saw John gain a few turns; I would add a few more degrees to my course to increase the angle to the fish. This little change made both the fish and the angler work harder. *(See Paralleling & Mirroring on p. 165, Chapter 20)*

The angle of the line as it entered the water, indicated the tuna was swimming near the surface and all three of us were hoping to catch sight of him. There was a splash as he decided he'd had enough of this parallel game. He turned south and headed for deep water again. All we saw was the white water from his decision to break away from the parallel attitude.

The rod doubled over and line started peeling off the spool again. John had both hands on the fore grip and was leaning well back, keeping the butt end at a 45° angle, as he repeatedly said, "Go boy, go boy, go boy!" I put the control lever in reverse, stopping our forward motion, and the fish began towing us backwards, directly toward the P-town monument, once again.

With a little over half the line off the spool, the peeling slowed and came to a halt. This time the line was at a steep angle and the fish was working his big butt off. John had sweat right through both his tee and his blue linen shirt.

"Now he's doing himself plenty of harm. You may be hot and

sweaty now, but your work is just beginning. Wait until your tuna is ready to be taken."

In the next 10 or 15 minutes, Bruce helped John remove his shirt and hat, poured ice water over his head and down his neck, and gave him a drink of Pepsi. John shrugged his shoulders and exclaimed, "You're one hell of a mate, Bruce!"

Shortly after John had his cold shower, the rod began to straighten. John glanced over his head at the bridge as if to say he was ready, and took three turns on the reel.

I watched John haul back on the rod and gain several more turns. "OK." I declared, "He's ready to be taken. From now on, it's your strength and your will to capture him, against his desire for freedom. Listen and do exactly what Bruce and I tell you to do."

When an angler can't continue to gain line with his back and arms alone, it's time to crank himself up, off the chair, and "ride" the bucket harness. This allows the angler to use his weight to increase the pressure on the fish as he leans back and lowers his butt into the fighting chair. Bruce didn't have to explain this procedure; John knew how to do it instinctively. All the mate had to say was, "Ride him, John, ride him!" and each time John would take several cranks on the reel and hike himself above the chair seat, lean back, sit down and put kinetic energy into the rod to winch our reluctant captive another foot closer to his demise. John was proving to be an excellent, experienced angler.

Twenty minutes of hiking with this pump-and-grind, and the spool was three quarters full. The angle to the fish had become much shallower and John was beginning to show signs of fatigue. With the fish up high again, the effort of towing *Misty* became easier. Bruce leaned close to John's ear and said, "Don't let him get his second wind. If he begins to dog it, give him a couple of sharp jabs. Let him know you're in charge."

John renewed his effort and again began gaining line. I turned the boat so the chair and rod were pointing to the starboard quarter, to induce the fish to swim somewhat parallel to our course. Bruce reminded John, "Be ready to just hold on when the tuna sees the boat and makes a last bid for its freedom." John nodded and said, "I want this bad bastard bad." Bruce followed with, "He's coming up." I countered with, "I can see the double line. He's about 100 feet off, now."

John had made 10 or 12 more turns of the handle when the fish broke clear of the surface, eyeballed *Misty*, splashed and streaked for the safety of deep water. John held on and was again riding the bucket harness, this time with the rod tip doubled over to the gunwale and throbbing with the determined effort of the quarry. John yelled, "I made eye contact with that magnificent creature and he doesn't like what we're doing to him! I love it, love it, love it!" It now looked as if the fish had set his feet and was swimming in tight circles trying to get to the bottom. When this happens the line is scribing a classic "cone." The line at the rod tip is the point of the cone while the circling fish is defining the rim.

This last desperate effort drained away much of the fish's energy, leaving him in the circling-mode with his only desire to resist the gradual rising toward the surface that he had fought so hard to leave.

The fish and angler were again in a balanced standoff. After a few minutes I was able to determine that the fish was circling counter-clockwise and was hooked on his left side, which meant he should be taken on our starboard side. *(See Special Gear & Tactics – Chapter 20)*

'When you feel his swimming action begin to slow down let Bruce and me know. Your fish is about 150 to 200 feet away. From here on, the battle is just a slow and steady retrieval of the line until Bruce can reach the double line, and wire him to the side for me to harpoon. Once Bruce has the line in hand, don't forget to back the drag off about halfway, in case the fish makes another run. We don't want to lose this guy because of a sudden snapping of the line. If your arms give out, Bruce or I can take over."

I heard John mumble something to the effect that my last

suggestion was "impossible. He's mine and I'm taking him all the way." To which Bruce countered, "Prove it."

John dropped into a steady "lift and crank:" routine that soon had the fish within 50 feet. The fish set his feet and refused to allow John to crank him any closer to the surface. I put a quarter turn to starboard on the wheel, slipped the control into forward at idle speed, and told John to hold on and not crank until our forward motion had planed the fish off our stern.

I took a quick look at the water around the boat. We were still alone, so I descended to the deck to make ready the cockpit harpoon. By the time I had it rigged and ready, Bruce had the double line in hand and was wiring the fish forward for me to stick.

When Bruce had half the double line in hand, he walked forward along the starboard side of the cockpit, bringing the fish to within five feet of my position at the starboard quarter. One thrust and then a push on the end of the cockpit harpoon drove the shank well into our quarry.

I held the spent fish with the harpoon line while Bruce gave the tail rope to John. John slipped the rope over the tail, cinched up the noose, and suddenly it was over. I glanced at my watch. It was just over an hour and 40 minutes since the hook-up.

Handshakes and congratulations went all around, followed by the *Misty* traditional round of Jim Beam and Pepsi.

After bleeding the fish, Bruce measured the length and girth, estimating the weight at approximately 810 pounds. (It weighed 795 lbs on the Green Harbor Tuna Club's official scale.)

During the clean up and preparation for our return to port, John climbed to the bridge and stared at his prize in disbelief and utter silence. He remained silent until we were more than halfway home.

Then, in a soft and gentle voice he said, "Now I know what separates the bluefin from all others. They may not be as fast, they don't jump or tail walk, and they're not as agile as many of the game fish I've caught, but no fish out there can match their power and stamina. They're like a runaway express train, hell-bent on their own destruction, and when they decide to run, nothing can stop them.'

After a short pause, he added, "My experience today was like no other I've ever had. Thanks to you and Bruce, this has been a really great day. THANK YOU BOTH!"

No argument from the crew. It had been a very good day, indeed!

Chapter 2

A half-century's brief history

The giant bluefin tuna fishery of the last half of the 20th century had many dynamic changes. Some of these changes had to do with the fish and the fishermen who pursued them, but the most profound changes were brought about by economics, government, advances in technology, changes in both national and international laws, world trade, and often, just downright greed.

Fishermen made changes in the way tuna were caught, whether for sport or for consumption by man, but at times both the recreational and commercial sectors had reason to wonder if they were catching or being caught themselves.

The '50s – The Start Up

The beginning of this decade saw only token activity by the recreational sector. Angling for these powerful speedsters was in its infancy. While most serious sportsmen-anglers were in pursuit of the mighty marlin and its spectacular acrobatics, there were only a few showing an interest in angling for tuna. It would take the rest of this decade for the tackle industry to develop equipment capable of handling the powerful bluefin.

The commercial fishery for bluefin was also in its infancy. Capt. Manny Phillips, in his *Silver Mink* out of Provincetown, was perfecting the methods for purse seining in the developing fishery. The demand for tuna as animal food was just beginning.

Humans had not yet developed a taste for the strong flavor of raw or cooked bluefin. In the United States that taste may never come about. The majority of our citizens settle for albacore and other bland species.

The '60s – Growing Pains & Growing Interest

This decade saw more changes in the recreational sector than in the commercial. Anglers became intrigued with the speed and raw power of the bluefin. Huge schools of bluefin were returning to the Cape Cod and Massachusetts Bay areas each season and on top of that, they were growing longer and stronger every year.

Good anglers always rise to a challenge and the tackle industry will always design new equipment to help them meet that challenge. By the end of this period, we see the development of larger and stronger reels, fiberglass rods, roller guides and tips. In addition, better fighting chairs, Dacron lines, monofilament lines, triple xxx hooks and a host of other new and exotic terminal gear came into play.

In the '60s, big reels like this Penn 16/0 became the standard.

By the late sixties, there may have been only ten or twelve boats actively targeting tuna in and around the Bay State waters. As word of this new fishery spread, the number began to change dramatically.

The '70s – High Times & High Crimes

Interest in bluefin fishing spread throughout the Atlantic coast as fishermen learned of the huge schools that had taken up seasonal residency in the Gulf of Maine. By 1973, it was not unusual to see boats from New Jersey, Maryland, Virginia and Florida trolling in the waters of Cape Cod Bay and Stellwagen Bank. I heard one Captain complaining to a friend, "Where in hell did all these foreigners come from? There must have been 35 boats on the SW corner of the Bank today!" No one had any idea that that number would expand to over 400 on a beautiful weekend day, in August of 1977 — just four years later!

The decade began with foreign vessels beginning to proliferate on Georges Bank, causing fishermen throughout the Gulf of Maine to ask the federal government to invoke a 200-mile limit for our territorial waters, as other governments, the world over, were doing. Our fishermen knew even then that the stocks were being depleted.

Although Manny Phillips started seining tuna in 1952 for a cannery in Maine, the commercial tuna industry is generally considered to have started in 1973, when a Japanese vessel, the *Tat Sumi Maru*, entered Portland Harbor, Maine, offering to buy bluefin at 20 cents a pound. The U.S. State Department was then against increasing our territorial waters from 12 NM to 200 NM.

In March 1974, the *Commercial Fisheries News* of Stonington, Maine reported that there were 322 foreign fishing vessels off the East coast of the United States.

At the end of 1975, the House of Representatives passed the 200-mile limit bill and sent it to the Senate. Finally, the Magnuson Fishery Conservation and Management Act (200-mile limit) was signed into law in April of 1976 by President Gerald Ford, just three months before our nation's Bicentennial celebration.

That was the year when the Japanese market began to grow. The Oriental taste for fresh, raw bluefin spawned a host of joint ventures between American fish dealers and Japanese buyers.

The going price at the beginning was 25 cents per pound, and by the end of the season, had risen to $1.25 — not nearly what it was to become in the early '90s, but significant enough to draw the attention of hordes of fishermen. After all, "a buck and a quarter a pound" for a fish that dressed out at 500 pounds, is not a bad day's pay!

By the end of the decade, that price had risen to as much as $10 per pound for a quality fish.

This 10-year period also saw the start of the fragmentation of the fishery. If you create a good "chum-soup" by combining these ingredients: rising economic opportunities, an abundant stock, easy access, inexpensive start-up costs, very low experience requirements, throw in a large portion of old-fashioned greed, and mix well with a heaping helping of government inefficiency, you are bound to have a fishery made up of user-groups fighting over allocations, instead of fighting for conservation.

The U.S. became a member of the International Commission for the Conservation of Atlantic Tunas (ICCAT). The International body was formed to oversee and protect the Atlantic tuna stocks from depletion. As a leading member of this organization, the U.S. has a say in forming International regulations and setting quotas for its member countries. Each member country agrees to carry out those regulations and stay within their individual quotas.

Each member country is left to develop its own regulations for dividing its quotas among the various user groups, in a fair and equitable manner. As William Shakespeare wrote: "Aye, there's the rub!"

If this sounds like a relatively easy task, you have never sat in on a public hearing having to do with any of the fisheries. Each user group has an idea of what its share of the quota should be, and can come up with logical reasons to receive that share. Needless to say, it would take a Solomon to devise a fair plan, and even then, the user groups would still be dissatisfied. In public hearings having to do with the tuna fishery, cool heads and civilized behavior usually gave way to angry shouting and rowdy actions. — Fragmentation Rules!

By the end of this decade, the equipment industry had developed the bent-butt, 2-speed reels, and line manufacturers had increased the strength of mono-line while at the same time decreasing its diameter.

The '80s – Growth & Control

This decade started with ICCAT placing restrictions on the quota allowed to the Western Atlantic tuna fishermen. In 1982, the quota was lowered from 7,000 metric tons to only 800 metric tons.

In 1983, the Fisheries Conservation Zone (FCZ) that was created when the 200-mile limit was passed became the Exclusive Economic Zone (EEZ), when President Ronald Reagan declared all waters within 200 NM of our coastlines to be a US sovereign area under control of the federal government.

By the mid-80s, tuna fishermen were disgusted with the regulatory mess by which they were controlled: ICCAT was setting world quotas that were completely ignored by non-member nations. The National Marine Fisheries Service (NMFS) was trying to divide the Western Atlantic quotas among the various categories (seiners, rod and reel, harpoon category, and general category) and at the same time, trying to split the quota between the areas north of Cape Cod and those south of the Cape. The problem became a nightmare of allocation, with almost total disregard for the status of the resource. Fishermen were pitted against fishermen. (NMFS seems able to do this quite well, no matter what fishery they are charged with managing.)

The value of the fishery continued to rise. The end of the decade saw $12 to $14 per pound price tags for quality tuna. With prices at this level, tuna fishing attracted almost everyone who owned a boat, whether it was able to make it to the grounds or not. As the decade closed, the NMFS had issued 23,000 tuna permits. (It has been estimated that 20,000 of those permits were never put to use. Of the remaining 3,000 permit holders, 2,000 probably never even hooked up, which leaves only about one thousand boats that may have landed at least one tuna. I remember seeing other statistics that proclaimed only four or five hundred permits had multiple catches to their credit!)

The '90s – Stock Assessment Fight & Economics

The re-authorization of the Magnuson Act has a provision to include all Highly Migratory Species (HMS) under its control. This may seem to be a good idea, but it is just one more government agency that has a say in the control of tuna management.

In 1991, the on-going controversy over stock assessments threatened to reduce the tuna fishery drastically. Both conservationists and NMFS advocated large cuts in quotas after scientists estimate the stock to be deleted. The East Coast Tuna Association (ECTA), an organization of tuna fishermen from Maine to New Jersey disagreed with that assessment and to prove their point, showed photos of huge schools of tuna on the surface over a large portion of the waters off the coasts of Maine, New Hampshire and Massachusetts — all taken on the same day. ECTA had again proved the old adage that "seeing is believing".

The year 1993 saw tuna fishermen catching their allotments easily and the price remained good, but the argument over stock levels continued to split management and fishermen. The following year, the general category fishery was closed on 14 August, the earliest closure ever.

The argument over stock levels continued to split management and fishermen throughout the 1993 season. An independent peer review of the stock by the National Academy of Science found no reduction in numbers of bluefin and came out in support of the one-stock theory. For years, biologists were divided; some thought the Western Atlantic tuna were a separate stock from those found along the European coast, while others argued for the one-stock theory.

Mid-decade brings a small increase in quota for the Western

Atlantic tuna-men, when ICCAT rejects a bid for a 40% decrease in overall quotas. The mid-Atlantic angling category was shut down in 1996 because popularity and huge numbers of fishermen overrode the quota.

ECTA sponsored the tagging of bluefin, with the newly developed pop-up tags designed to detach from their host tuna at intervals of up to three months from the date of the tagging. The successful results of this 1997/1998 program showed the one-stock theory to be valid.

The weak Japanese economy in 1998 was felt by the American tuna fishermen, as prices plunged to levels paid in the early '80s. During this decade, the Japanese fish evaluators working with their American tuna dealers became much more discriminating about the quality of the fish. Temperature, fat content, color, smell and taste all go into the evaluation of the meat, resulting in a much wider price range offered for bluefin at the dock.

The commercial fishermen soon learn how to make sure they bleed properly and clean and cool the flesh as soon as the fish is taken, to insure a better product for the buyer and incidentally increase the profit for the boat that brought the product to market.

In most ports, when a fish is brought in, there is intense competition between the dealers, which gives the fisherman a chance to sell to the highest bidder. What a change: the angler can now bargain for the best offer instead of having to accept a "take it or leave it" deal. As with the medical profession, a second opinion can be a benefit to the patient/angler.

The last year of the century saw an upturn in the Japanese economy, but the high value for premium bluefin did not return to the level seen in the mid-'90s.

The last tuna season of the century had one very encouraging circumstance. The appearance of multitudes of "football" tuna, not quite big enough to take legally, elicited strong reactions within the tuna community. Some members were frustrated because they had to free their catch, while others were delighted to see a fresh, young stock becoming "imprinted" to local waters. The prevailing opinion seemed to be the same as the avid Red Sox fan – "Wait 'til next year!"

The bad news is that the decade ended with fishermen and government managers still at odds with each other over the allocation and management regulations.

The European Community tried to change the interpretation of a '98 agreement on bluefin quotas for the Eastern Atlantic in an attempt to *hide* recent bluefin overruns by its member countries, and allow the EC to increase its quota without penalty for the overage. The U.S. and Canadian delegations held firm. The bottom line: The U.S. agreed not to force the penalties issued for the EC and the EC dropped its demands for a quota rollover.

I hope that last paragraph is completely clear to the reader. If it isn't clear, and it seems like gobbledygook to you, you are not alone. Please don't call me – it doesn't really make sense to me either. It is typical of some governments to try to reinterpret agreements, as though they were etched in stone, if one of the signees thinks it can gain an advantage. They will turn the stone not only into sand, but find a willing nation with a large empty receptacle in which to pound it up!

The good news is that the large numbers of small fish that showed up throughout the area seem to indicate a high level of recruitment.

The ups and downs seen, especially in the last 30 years, the proliferation of regulations imposed by NMFS and ICCAT, the problems of allocation of quotas, the in-fighting between fishermen from various categories, the wide value swings of the market – all brought about by the two strongest driving forces in the fishing community, or should I say world community – economics and just plain greed, seem bound to continue well into the 21th century.

A Look Forward — The 21st Century

The new stock seems to be healthy and as these new recruits grow larger and stronger each succeeding year, this fishery will continue to be the most interesting, most complicated, most intriguing, most exciting, and as always, the most challenging fishery of them all.

If that last statement seems a little overly didactic, I would suggest the reader ask any angler they know, who has "been there, done that," for *their* opinion. In which case, I don't believe you will need to seek a second one.

The Battleground

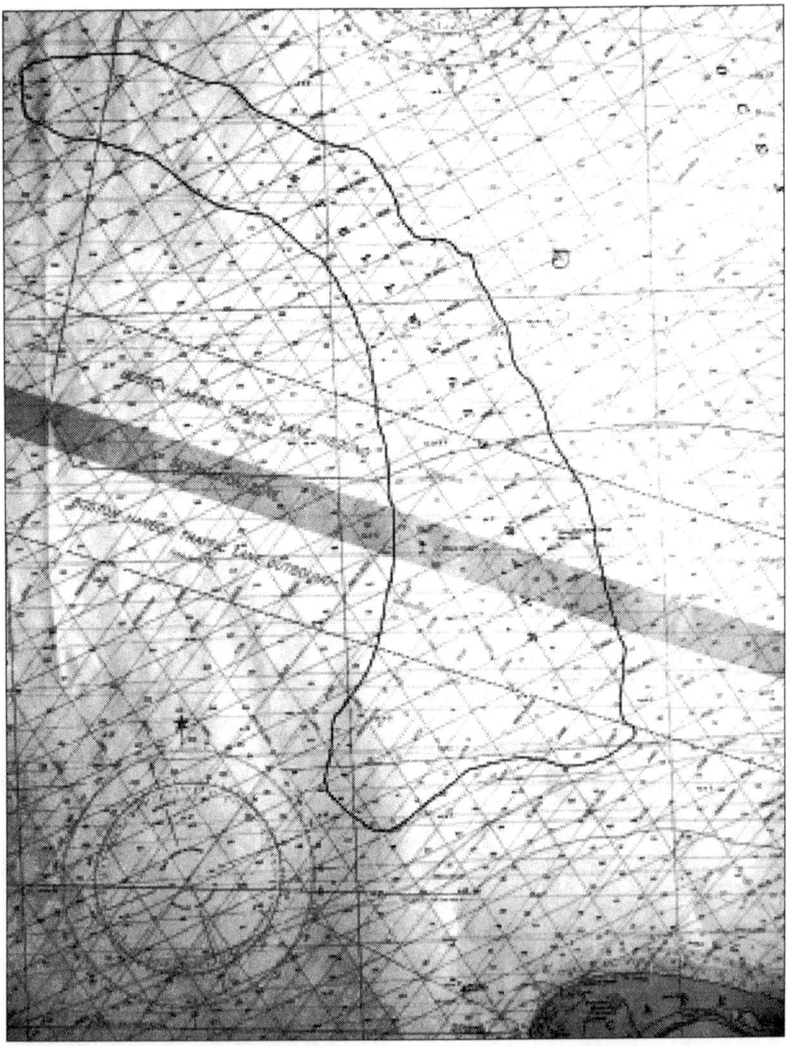

Bluefin tuna range the whole of Stellwagen Bank, (the boomerang shape on this chart excerpt). The northwest and southwest corners are the usual hot spots.

Chapter 3

The First One: Almost Lost The Boat

Before the sun peeked over the horizon, the sky was a mass of pink, red and purple hues reflecting off the thick clouds in the east. I was parked next to Charlie's Famous Clam Shack overlooking Cape Cod Bay in the Brant Rock section of Marshfield, Mass. I rolled down the window of my pickup as the sun pulled itself free of the horizon and I noticed the breeze from the east was beginning to freshen. I checked the time, – 0545 – put the pickup in gear and headed for Green Harbor Marina. Something kept running through my mind: "Red sky in the morning, sailor take warning."

A few minutes later I pulled up to the pier where the new 29-foot Dwyer, with its fighting chair and custom-made tuna rods, was waiting to make its first trip to Stellwagen Bank. The crew, Ray, (my mate), Jack and David had arrived 15 minutes early and already were busy getting *Misty* ready. All I had to do was start the engine, drop her into gear and head down the harbor.

As *Misty* cleared the east jetty, I swung the wheel to port and the bow came around into a nasty three-foot chop. The breeze had freshened to a steady 15 knots out of the east. Half an hour later, halfway to the SW corner of Stellwagen Bank, I turned the VHF radio to the weather channel.

" ... from Eastport to Block Island, out to 25 nautical miles; small craft warnings have been posted, winds from the east at 15 to 25 knots..."

When I squinted into the spray, I could see some images on the horizon. It looked like the fleet was on its way home, and I was thinking much along the same lines.

"Hey fellas, it looks like the fleet has called it a day. I think we ought to abort today and try again after the blow." Hearing no answer from below, I looked into the cockpit and saw the crew earnestly working on some leader cable. They were sewing an egg-sinker weight into the throat of a gutted mackerel. I could see the business end of a tuna hook protruding from the anal cavity.

I pulled the throttle back to 1500 RPMs to make the going easier, and twenty minutes later the radio crackled. "Hey, Cap. It's wild out there – all the boats that were anchored near the notch are headed for the barn. You might want to turn around. Over."

"Thank you for that. We'll be right behind you," I replied. I looked back into the cockpit, noticed the crew had sought the shelter of the salon, and yelled from the bridge, "Okay, that's it. We're going home."

Dave stuck his head out into the spray. "How far to the Bank?" It seemed this crew always answers a statement with a question. "We're about five minutes from the notch," I answered, referring to the underwater indentation cut into the side of the steep rise leading to the plateau-like SW corner of the Bank.

Dave came back with, "Let's give it ten minutes, Cap. We have a fresh-sewn mack ready to troll." "OK. I can see an anchor ball about a mile ahead. I'm going to swing around it and when we're clear, I want lines in and all the gear stowed. It's going to be a tough trip home." I dropped to 900 RPMs and watched as Dave put the single sewn bait into the wake, and placed the rod in the trolling arm of the fighting chair.

As we approached the notch, the seas became steeper and closer together. "We have got to be nuts!" I said to myself, as "Red sky in the morning" kept running through my mind.

When the depth began to rise on the paper machine, I headed for the anchor ball, about a hundred yards ahead. I could make out the Provincetown Monument about eight nautical miles SSE of our position and almost in line with the anchor ball.

"Hooked-up, Cap! We're hooked-up!" Dave screamed from below. "The fish is headed toward the P'town Monument. Turn her to port!"

I gunned the engine and turned the rudder to port to avoid getting hung up on the anchor ball. As it slid past the starboard side, I saw David lift the rod as high as he could, raising the line out of the water enough so it passed over the ball, instead of snagging the anchor ball and cutting the quarry free. It sure helps to have crewmembers on the same page when the situation demands instant action.

Jack put on the bucket harness, sat in the chair and with the rod placed in the gimbal, was ready for the fight.

I brought *Misty* to a course that put us parallel to the fish, about 100 yards to starboard, and increased the speed to match that of the fish. After ten minutes of this kind of pressure, our quarry slowed and Jack began to pump the rod to let him know that we were not going to give him a chance to rest.

The fish began changing course, more to the east, forcing me to do likewise, and it soon had *Misty* with her stern into the seas. "We'll stay in this attitude and see how he likes towing us into the sea stern first," I yelled. I saw Jack lean back into the chair enabling him to hold the rod as a good 60-degree angle.

As the transom met each succeeding sea, water came over the stern and began soaking the angler and crew. Caught up in the excitement of the battle, they seemed not to notice and were soon soaked through to the skin. A few minutes later, I noticed that both Dave and Ray were working the cockpit in ankle-deep water. Thank God for the watertight decks and the scuppers.

After ten minutes of this towing-stern-to, Jack was able to pump the rod and begin to gain some line. Suddenly, the rod tip began to vibrate and Jack said, "I think we've got him tail-wrapped." I looked at the spool; it was over half-full.

Jack was now reeling in line at a steady pace, and I was about to ask Ray to make ready the tail rope when he emerged from the cabin carefully coiling it. "We're still on the same page," I thought to myself, as he put the bitter end through the hawsepipe and secured it to the cleat under the gunwale.

When the double line reached the rod tip, we could see the exhausted fish with his left gill-plate held closed by the leader cable trailing down his left side and making one turn around each lobe of his tail. David grabbed the double line and began hauling in the last 30 feet. Ray slipped the noose over the tail, and as a cheer went up, I put *Misty* in gear and turned the wheel hard to port.

As she came around into the trough, she heeled over much more than usual. "Hold on!" I screamed, as I hit the throttle to bring the bow into the wind. It was all too apparent that she had taken on water! I looked over the port side and noticed with relief that the bilge pump was working.

I asked Jack to take the wheel as Dave lifted the engine box and I descended from the bridge. The water was halfway up the engine, covering both batteries and the starter. If *Misty* had been powered with gasoline, the engine would have shorted out and we would be caught in these rough seas with a dead boat. [Lesson one: a water-tight deck isn't much good when water can run down the companionway into the cabin.]

Ray said, "I noticed it was up to my knees when I went in to get the tail rope." As the crew looked at him with a "why the hell didn't you say something?" expression, he added, "First things first." And went aft to bleed the fish.

An hour and forty-five minutes had passed since we hooked up. Jack kept *Misty* headed into the seas at idle until the bilge was pumped out and the fish was bled. While Jack handled the boat, the rest of us went about cleaning the cockpit and stowing the loose gear.

"Now…first things first," I declared as I broke out the Jim Beam and Pepsi. As congratulations were passed around, we first toasted the fish and then Father Neptune for allowing us to take it before we foundered and sank. (I later realized just how close we came, and how important respect for and knowledge of the sea can factor into our very survival.)

The next task proved to be very tedious: How do you get a line through each gill and secure the fish to the stern for towing headfirst, when seas are six to eight feet high? The first attempt, into the seas at idle, was aborted because the stern and the fish were not rising and falling together, making it impossible to even get a line down the throat. The second attempt, down wind and sea, proved to be much too dangerous as the surging of the boat and fish would have resulted in broken limbs for the crew, when the fish and stern came together. The third option, straight down the troughs and crests, proved to be manageable, now that the bilge had been pumped dry and *Misty* was again seaworthy.

Soon, with the fish secured for towing in the headfirst mode, we were underway to our harbor.

As we began the two-hour trip to the west, the sun reappeared and the wind and seas let go. I glanced down from the bridge at the fish riding on the first wake and smiled with appreciation at the great job the crew had done under very adverse conditions.

My smile stretched into a grin as I saw the crew, in their underwear, hanging the rest of their clothing from any place they could find. There was even a pair of dungarees flying from the port yardarm. The crew was taking advantage of the automatic "blow-dry" effect created by *Misty's* easy-going 10 knot advance toward the barn! We must have looked like a Chinese junk on its way up the Hwang-Poo River, headed for Shanghai.

As we entered the harbor and slowed to headway speed, the crew, now fully dressed in their still-damp clothes, put over the fenders, rigged the dock lines and began to turn the fish tail-first to facilitate the off-loading. As we approached the marina, I let go one long blast, and was answered by a chorus of bells, whistles and shouts. (The year was 1972. Tuna fishing was still pursued for the sport of it and the pride of accomplishment gained from a task well done.)

After the weigh-in and the obligatory snap-shots, I overheard someone in the crowd talking to Ray. "Gee, you guys must have had a tough time catching that fish, what with the wind at 25 knots and the seas up to eight to ten feet!" Ray looked the gentleman in the eye, and with his typical affinity for understatement, replied, "No problem."

Epilogue:

This fish weighed in at 603 pounds, whole weight. It dressed out at 468 pounds and was sold to the Purina Corporation for cat food at 5 cents per pound. – Return: $23.40.

Expenses:
Diesel – 20 gals @ 27¢ per gal. = $5.40
Crew = $0.00
Rebuild water damaged starter = $85.00
Total = $90.40

The net cost for the day was $67. (Remember: this was 1970). Today, with the cost of fuel, bait and tackle, you are looking at an expense of over $200 – just to spend a day "tuna-wishing".

If this fish had been taken in the late '80s, it could have brought in as much as $20 per pound, and been worth $9,360!

When I think back to this day, the net expense of sixty-seven bucks is not bad for a great experience and the thrill that comes with your first giant bluefin!

Chapter 4

The 2nd One & The Charter

What a difference a couple of days can make. Lazy, gentle swells, two to three feet in height, were rolling from the NE. With the wind speed at zero, the glassy surface of the undulations reminded me of the mirrors I used to see in the funhouse, when I was growing up and spending most of my summer nights in the Arcades on the boardwalk in Ocean City, NJ.

It was two days after the *Misty* crew had caught their first tuna in eight to ten foot seas, with wind approaching 25 knots. *Misty* was again on the SW corner of Stellwagen Bank, looking for number two. I had no charter lined up, so Ray (the mate) and I decided to try our luck at meat fishing again. Jack was back at work, so Ray asked Dave to go, and he was aboard as a third helping hand.

We had arrived at our LORAN coordinates at about 0630. We set the anchor, hung our hook baits under their balloons and settled into the "chop and plop" mode.

As the hours pass without any action, the senses begin to dull and the powers of concentration disappear, just as surely as stripers do when the water temperature drops to the low fifties. Dave was on "automatic" with the chum ladle, Ray was asleep in the chair, and I was thinking about the swordfish steak I had been promised for supper.

Oddly enough, the muffled sound of a bait balloon popping under the water made no impression on either Dave or me, but Ray came out of the chair, fully awake, grabbed the rod and set the hook. "Hooked-up, hooked-up, Cap!"

Dave began clearing the other lines while I started the engine and pulled the quick release on the anchor ball. Ray was braced against the transom, keeping the tip as high as the fish and the drag system would allow. *Misty* began to gain sternway to the west.

As soon as we cleared the fleet, Ray reminded me that I had decided it was to be my turn in the chair, all the way, for the second fish. Dave came to the bridge to handle the boat and I jumped to the cockpit, placed the bucket harness on the chair and sat down. Ray stuck the rod's butt in the gimbal and helped me snap the harness to the reel. As soon as Ray allowed the pressure he was holding against the fish to be transferred to my arms and legs, I had my first idea of the power of these creatures. I suddenly knew what experienced tuna men had told me, "Until you have reeled in a giant, there is no way you can understand just what they are about." There is no substitute for hands-on experience, and since I was entering the tuna fishery, I needed to gain the basic angler experience. When talking to successful tuna anglers you will only get a vicarious variety of impressions not likely to be very vivid and in many cases purely purposeful prevarications. Although I had "been there," until now I had never "done that."

The fish continued to tow *Misty* slowly toward the west at a very steep angle. It seemed as if he was more interested in trying to get to the bottom than he was in towing the boat. The angle at which the line enters the water is a good indication of how hard the fish has to work to tow the boat. My adversary was working very hard, so there was no reason to change our M.O., as long as he stayed that deep.

Another 10 minutes of this balance of pressure and he decided to change tactics and began to swim toward the surface. As the down angle of the line decreased, he was able to increase the towing speed with less effort on his part.

I was beginning to think about what our next move should be, when Ray said it looked as if we were going to get a chance to see our adversary. The angle continued to decline. Dave called down from his vantage point on the bridge, saying that he could see the fish's "V" wake and that he should be completely visible very soon.

When he reached the surface, about two football fields away, he was still swimming strongly to the west. I was able to hold the tip almost straight up. In this mode, the line was out of the water for at least half the distance to the fish.

Ray and I had just decided to try to parallel the fish on its left, so it would have to work harder to pull the line through the water. (pulling 200 yards of tuna line sideways instead of end-on is like towing a plywood sheet through the water, flat side to.) Dave interrupted, "I don't want to cause you any concern, but have you seen what's approaching from the north?"

Our eyes soon focused on a shark fin slicing slowly through the water in a southerly direction, half way between the fish and the boat. As the fin's distance to the line decreased, it was evident that the shark was beyond where the line entered the water. Dave and I became transfixed, both of us waiting for the dorsal fin to part our only connection to the bluefin.

Just before the fin reached the line, Ray unhooked the bucket buckles, grabbed the rod from my hands and raised it high over his head. The extra lift and the increase in tension resulted in a few more feet of airborne line.

We watched as the tip of the fin just tweaked the line and the shark passed safely underneath. Dave and I expelled air from our lungs with a sound like a truck makes when it releases its air brakes. Ray nonchalantly placed the rod back in the gimbal and hooked the bucket buckles to the reel. "No problem, Cap. Now, let's take this fish."

Dave brought the bow around to parallel the fish at a distance of about 100 yards to starboard. As the tension increased, I adjusted the drag to keep the balance of power. Each time the fish started to dog it, I'd give him a few "jabs" by jerking the rod to prod him into more activity, preventing him from getting his second wind.

Ten minutes of this increased effort and he began to give way toward the boat. Dave compensated equally with the helm each time the fish made a move, and I was able to gain a few feet of line.

"Let's see if he is ripe for the picking. Turn her hard to the right and take her out of gear. Let's see how he likes the towing mode now." Dave followed my suggestion and soon we were stern to tail. This time the progress was at a much slower pace. It was obvious to me that both of us were tiring. The only question in my mind was, "which one of us has the strongest will?" I could almost feel the resolve draining from the fish's desire to be free of his antagonists. Taking note of the fish's weakening struggle, Ray said, "The ball's in your court now. Crank him in so I can stick him. You want to tail wrap him, don't you? Get to it and do it!"

I had closed the distance to less than 100 feet, when the fish realized the balance of power had shifted in our favor. He decided we were getting too close and immediately took off most of the line I had taken in. As the line was peeling off, Ray yelled, "You got him now! Pump and crank, pump and crank!" At this point, I was hot, sweaty and my adrenaline tank was depleted. All I could muster in response was an exhausted, "Yeah, right."

At the end of this run, the fish slowed down and seemed to give in. I began to feel I had finally put a slam-dunk through the hoop to tie the game. Now it was up to me to sink a three-pointer to win the game.

With a new shot of energy, I began working the fish in the classic style, by lifting the rod tip and then cranking until I was riding the harness above the chair seat, then leaning back and sitting down to increase the bow and the kinetic energy imparted to the rod.

The repeated jabbing at the fish, each time I sat down, seemed to be eroding his stamina. The question was again, "which one of us had the stronger will?" I really wanted this fish, but my desire could not stack up against an enemy that was literally fighting for his life. This thought caused a wave of weariness. As my pace slowed, Ray's urging became more insistent.

Suddenly, the line went slack. "He's charging the boat! Put it in forward and goose it!," I yelled, as I began cranking as fast as my fatigue would allow. Dave threw it in gear, hit the throttle and *Misty* leaped forward. I paused long enough to loosen the drag half way so the shock of the line becoming taut would not snap it, or pull the hook.

Before I could resume cranking, the rod tip went over and the spool began backing off. Dave dropped the RPMs to the point where *Misty* was just keeping a slight towing pressure on our opponent.

About 15 minutes of very slow winching brought my energy level to "E" for exhaustion. "Okay, Cap. Keep going, here comes the double line. We're only 45 feet from him. Give it 15 or 20 more turns." As Ray said this, he positioned himself under the rod at the transom, ready to hand-line the leader.

With two or three turns of double line on the reel, Ray began to work hand-over-hand, and Dave came down from the bridge to make ready the cockpit harpoon.

One thrust and suddenly it was over. I placed the tail-rope over the tail fins and cinched it tight.

While Ray was bleeding the fish by raking the gills with the shank of the harpoon, Dave and I began to clean up and make ready to pick up our anchor ball and anchor. Another twenty minutes and we were underway to the harbor. The whole process, from the time of hook-up, had taken nearly two hours.

As soon as we pulled into the slip, I made some phone calls to arrange for the sale of the fish. Each call was answered with a loud negative. The domestic market was flooded and the cat-food buyer was unwilling to offer even 5 cents a pound! I returned to the boat and told Ray the bad news.

We decided to take the fish out to the nearby lobster grounds so it would at least become food for the local fish and crustaceans. It was mutually agreed that we would do this on our way to Race Point with tomorrow's charter customers who were flying in from the Mid-west for a day of bluefish fishing.

When Ray arrived the next morning, we secured the towing

lines to the cleats so the fish was hanging down about six feet below the water line, out of sight and, by mutual agreement, out of mind.

The members of the day's charter could be heard almost as soon as they drove into the parking area. The sounds that were drifting down the length of the pier were composed of the usual chatter of anticipation and remarks about the weather, the sea condition, the pool for the biggest fish, etc. Ray gave me a big wink as he welcomed them aboard. There was hardly any break in the dialogue as Ray stored their gear and we all exchanged first names.

We got underway and made way toward the harbor entrance at idle speed. As Ray stowed the lines and fenders, I noticed that he took a glance over the transom to see if the fish was visible. He came forward and told me, "At this speed, the fish is not planing enough to be seen."

As we continued down the harbor, the passengers broke out the coffee and donuts, and passed them all around with never a pause in the conversation.

If anything, the talk increased in intensity as we approached the seaward end of the jetty. I noticed they had gathered around the live-bait well, discussing the day and collecting the pool money. When *Misty* cleared the east jetty, I brought the bow around to the course for Race Point and hit the throttle.

In short order, the fish was riding the first wake, mouth open, with head and shoulders above the crest. Ray and I waited for the first man to look aft.

Minutes went by as they wolfed down the donuts and drained their thermoses. The designated keeper of the pool money gathered the bills and turned toward the stern. "What the hell is that?," he exclaimed as the currency went up in the air. In the next few seconds, the cockpit sole became a coffee, donut and paper cup mess as the charter members jostled each other, lunging for the transom for a better look.

Ray didn't bother to answer the query, but instead activated the wash-down pump and asked the charterers to please move forward, so he could clean up the slippery mess they had caused.

When he finished the clean up, the keeper of the pool stuffed the sticky, soaked bills into his pocket and asked Ray what kind of fish we were towing.

Ray broke into his signature broad grin, pointed to the bluefin and said, "That's a bluefish, and that's what we're going after, today. I doubt if we'll get one that big, though."

Nothing more needed to be said.

Capt. Roger's rod and reel bluefin tuna weighed 730 pounds.

Chapter 5

Bluefin Profile: Anatomy, Attributes, Antics

Bluefin tuna (*Thunnus thynnus*) is the largest member of the mackerel family and also the largest living species of bony fish. Some members of the shark family become larger than bluefin, but they are entirely cartilaginous. The only other living sea creatures larger than the bluefin are the great whales, which are mammals, not fish.

The International Game Fish Association (IGFA) all-tackle world record is 1,496 pounds. Ken Fraser, took this giant on 26 October, 1979 in Aulds Cove, Nova Scotia, Canada. A mere four pounds more and Fraser would have angled three quarters of a ton of fighting fury with only 130 lb test line! When I think about his unprecedented feat, I give him a tip-of-my-hat, and of course, award him the extra four pounds! I have seen tuna well into the 1,200s (my own personal record stands at an even 1,000 lbs), and believe me, these are very large creatures. When fully mature, some are almost 11 feet in length and have a girth of over 100 inches.

Bluefin are a highly migratory species. Fish that were tagged in the Bahamas have been recaptured as far north as Newfoundland and as far south as Uruguay.

Doctor Frank Mather

In September, 1977, I went to the Northeast Fisheries Science Center in Woods Hole, Mass., to report an albino bluefin tuna, that I had sighted about four nautical miles east of Hummarock, Mass. The receptionist immediately sent me to the Marine Laboratory, where I met Frank Mather, the leading biologist/fisherman specializing in tuna research. Dr. Mather had boated over 800 bluefin tuna. He always insisted on two criteria when he was the angler: all tackle must be ICFA regulation gear and all fish are to be released, unharmed. These two criteria made Dr. Mather a member of a very exclusive fellowship of ONE. In thirty years of fishing for tuna, I haven't ever heard of anyone who even *wanted* to become a member of that group.

He didn't ask why I was there because he was so excited about a tag from a tuna he had just received that day. The fish had been tagged in the Bahamas and had been recaptured off the coast of Norway. Dr. Mather had factored in the probability that the fish had followed the Gulf Stream in its journey, and thus covered a distance of some 5,000 nautical miles. The fact that this tuna had been caught only 50 days after being tagged meant it had swum an average of 100 miles per day. The fish had lost some 65 pounds during its journey. (Fish often live off the energy stored in their bodies when they are unable to find food.) Dr. Frank believed that this tuna might have run amuck in the true sense of the word. (Webster's dictionary gives two definitions for amuck: one is to "rush about in a frenzy to kill," and the other is "to lose control of oneself and do or attempt violence.") Why any creature runs amuck is still a strange mystery

After finishing his tale of the tagged tuna, the good doctor apologized for his excited state and finally asked me why I had come to see him. I told him about the albino tuna sighting and he was once again elated. He wanted to know every detail about the sighting; the who, when, where and how, the estimated size, the actions, coloring, any distinguishing markings, and anything unusual when compared to a normal bluefin. His intensity, fervor and thoroughness, and yes, his charms made it clear why he had become the world's leading authority on bluefin tuna. As with most fish, all members of the mackerel family are carnivores. Their diet consists of eels, squid, a variety of crustations and fish, including mackerel, flying fish, butter fish, mullet, herring, whiting, flounder, and bluefish. They have often been observed jumping clear of the water, with bluefish scattering everywhere in an attempt to escape.

Anatomy

Being the largest member of the mackerel family, bluefin are extremely streamlined. They have a bullet-shaped nose and a caudal peduncle (the stalk-like part between the abdomen and the tail) that tapers sharply, almost to a point, before giving way to the larger vertical tail with its deep concaved V-shape. Just forward of the tail, on the peduncle, are its two horizontal diving planes (caudal keel) that control the fish's up and down attitude, much like the ailerons on the horizontal trailing section of an airplane tail.

Bluefin tuna are gunmetal blue/black on the top half and sometimes this upper half will show a hint of an iridescent gray/green. The bottom half is a silvery-white that often exhibits a mottled look with faint gray bands or spots. When freshly caught, the lower body lights up and radiates a beautiful blue, green and pinkish iridescence.

There are two dorsal fins; the forward one being the larger of the two with 12 or 14 spines that give it a shape much like the dorsal fin of a swordfish. The pectoral and pelvic fins are rather small for the size of the body. All of the fins are very dark, almost a black-brown. From the aft dorsal fin and the anal fin to the tail, there are eight bright yellow finlets with black tips, on both top and bottom of the caudal peduncle. All in all, the bluefin tuna is a beautiful and very colorful sea creature.

Attributes

Bluefin have a rapid growth rate; many reach a weight of 10 pounds at age one, and by age five some will be in the 100-pound range. Fish weighing over 600 pounds are estimated to be about age 14. I have found these "teenage" fish (600 – 700 lbs) to be frisky and have an abundance of stamina that we often see in their human counterparts. Bluefin over 800 pounds are no longer teenagers; they may have lost their youthful friskiness, but don't underestimate their raw strength and stamina.

Life expectancy is considered to be 25 to 28 years. These senior citizens of the Atlantic Ocean can be over 900 pounds and, except for the weight, they are generally easier to bring to gaff than the 600 or 700-pound teenagers. When it comes to using a flying-gaff to land a bluefin, my first suggestion is: "Don't use it." Opt for a cockpit harpoon instead. (See p. 157, Chapter 24) The largest tuna caught in Massachusetts's waters, by rod and reel, weighed 1,228 pounds and was just over 11 feet in length. This capture was in the late 1960s.

Bluefin are capable of attaining a speed of some 30 knots. (The equivalent of 35 mph in land miles.) This fact makes them one of the fastest animals on earth, in or out of the water. Their acceleration rate rivals that of drag racers; they explode from an idle to full speed in a matter of two or three seconds. (This sudden acceleration becomes very apparent when you miss a throw with the harpoon, and the resultant explosion thoroughly soaks the thrower on the pulpit-stand about 10 feet above the water where the fish *used to be.*)

Tuna have three unique attributes that give them a distinct advantage when it comes to speed, strength and stamina.

• First: Olympic swimmers either shave their heads or wear a tight fitting cap to eliminate drag in the water caused by hair, much like weed growth on a hull can slow a boat by one or two knots. Bluefin have no hair to slow them, but the dorsal fin with its spines can cause quite some drag, even when folded down. To give them an extra edge in speed, they have developed, through evolution, a smooth pocket into which they can completely tuck the dorsal, so it has no drag at all when they are in overdrive.

• Second: Olympic swimmers are trained to eliminate as much roll as possible from their stroke, because roll takes away some of their straight-forward progress. Tuna developed their finlets so they could eliminate roll completely. When the tail moves to the left, it imparts right-hand torque to the body, which results in roll. To compensate for the torque, the finlets on the top of the peduncle move to the right while those on the bottom move to the left. The reverse is true when the tail moves to the left. This finlet motion eliminates the roll, which allows all the energy generated by the peduncle and tail to direct the body straight ahead with no heel or yaw. Did these guys know a straight line is the shortest distance from here to there before Sir Isaac Newton?

• Third: Olympic swimmers might as well forget this third attribute. Bluefin have an extra organ used specifically as a heat exchanger. It is responsible for their strength and stamina when they are in an excitable or stressful state. This sausage-shaped organ can contain up to five or six quarts of blood and is located laterally just below the spinal column, adjacent to the stomach. This location, in cold-blooded animals, is the warmest area of the body. Some biologists question whether tuna are truly cold-blooded.

Each end of this heat exchanger has a valve, one is for filling, and one is for emptying. Under normal conditions, the organ is full and both valves are closed and the heart pumps the rest of the blood to the muscles using a built-in by-pass artery to avoid the "sausage." The blood in the heat exchanger reacts to its location and becomes as warm as any part of the body can. The blood that bypasses the organ disburses much of the body heat when it reaches the skin area, helping to maintain a temperature close to that of the surrounding environment.

When humans are under stress or frightened, the body receives a shot of adrenalin into the blood stream that heightens their physical alertness and strength. When a tuna becomes threatened, their number-one priority is to take a defensive posture or to use their speed to escape the threat. Under any stressful condition, the heat exchanger valves open and the heart pumps the warm whole blood throughout the body. The results is an animal with quickly warmed muscles, able to work at maximum efficiency, at top speed, and with more stamina and staying power than any other creature of the deep. Just think what speeds human athletes could attain if they had a built-in heat exchanger to augment their adrenalin surges? How about a two-minute mile? This would mean humans could run as fast as bluefin are able to swim!

Antics

Bluefish are one of the fastest fish in the sea; this speed combined with very quick and agile movements gives them a measure of protection from tuna. This fact seems to have created competition between the two species. As mentioned above, bluefish have been observed leaping out of the water followed closely by a pursuing tuna. Tuna are faster and could easily win any straight-ahead race, but bluefish don't often engage in a track meet. Instead, bluefish depend on their agility to escape capture. They remind me of a good broken-field runner that can fake the fastest defensive-back right out of his jock. When ever I see bluefish jumping clear of the the surface, I get the impression they are showing off their natural evasive abilities, just to tease and taunt the pursuing tuna. I personally have never seen a successful capture of a free-swimming bluefish by a tuna, when they are both in their element. As far as I know the only bluefish that have been caught by a tuna were those being live-lined or trolled on a daisy-chain or bar-rig.

Intellect

Don't ever underestimate the intelligence of tuna. When you are hooked up to one of these amazing fish, especially when using regulation IGFA tackle, your first thought should never be, "I'm going to outdo and out-muscle this beast." Instead, you should start planning a strategy to out-smart your adversary; because this is just what hooked tuna are planning to do to you!

Tuna try every trick in the book: dive for the bottom, try to strip all the line off the reel, change directions, charge the boat, surface to check out their antagonist, circle an anchor line to gain a purchase, and a host of other tricks. Just when you think you have seen it all, they come up with a new maneuver that can even dumbfound the high-liners. Their repertory of evasive actions seem to be passed on from generation to generation, which brings up the old controversy – is it hereditary or environmental? In this case, I believe it's a whole lot of both.

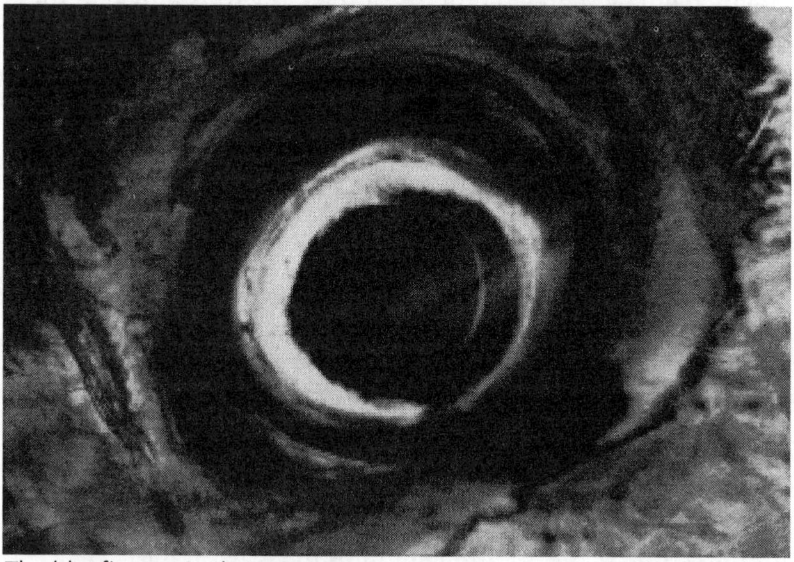

The bluefin tuna's observant eye

Stamina

Of the three outstanding characteristics of tuna, speed, strength and stamina, stamina is the one I marvel at the most. These guys will just not give up. After expending enough energy to drive *Misty* from P-town to Boston and back in the first hour of a fight for survival; a tuna will "set its feet" and absolutely not allow itself to be brought any closer than 30 or 40 feet to its human enemies. It prefers to use its weight and power to seek the protection of the depth while circling straight down under the boat.

I remember one such stand off when the fish literally almost exhausted three crewmembers and myself, remaining just beyond harpoon range for the better part of a half hour.

Misty had to get a jump-start that morning, but we figured the trip to the grounds would be sufficient to charge the batteries. Wrong. When the hook-up came, *Misty's* engine would not turn over. We had to try to land this fish with no help from the boat. Getting the quarry within 50 feet was a matter of only 40 minutes. It was the next half hour when our adversary "set his feet" and refused to be brought any closer than 30 or 40 feet to its human enemies. Three members of the crew took a turn at the handline, and each time, the tuna would take back what little gain they were able to attain. Finally the "big guy" grabbed the line and said: "Let me show you guys how to get this fish up to within sticking range." He had gained about 20 feet when the fish decided that was enough and returned to the safety of 40 feet — three or four times — before "big guy" gave it a salute and joined the rest of the exhausted crew.

It was time for a decision: either we would get Mr. Tuna close enough to stick, or he would break off and win the battle. I had the three crewmembers put the gangion over their shoulders and walk into the cabin, literally winching our enemy a good 25 feet closer to the surface. The gangion and leader held up under the added strain of being scraped over the rub-rail and gunwale, and I was able to get a good shot with the cockpit harpoon.

This tough teenage male weighed 685 lbs and Johnny Lima summed up the impression we all gained from the day's fishing in three words, "What unbelievable stamina!"

Bluefin and Orca

Robert Benchly will never write – *"Jaws VII – Killer whales save the entire population of Amity by attacking the great white menace."* – because he knows any drama that makes a "Free Willy" look aggressive will not fly.

(*Editor's note*: Also, Sea World would sue if tourism plummeted because people realized the lovable "Shamu" was a ruthless killer!)

There are only two living creatures capable of hunting down and killing bluefin. Orca, the killer whale, and good old Homo sapiens. Of these two enemies, mankind is by far the dominant predator. The only threat to the bluefin that shares its environment is the killer whale.

Orcas are toothed whales that attain a length of 25 feet and can weigh several tons. Their kind, gentle and entertaining interactions with mankind in the controlled environment of captivity completely belies their nature when they are free and in charge of their own destiny. In the wild, they often hunt in packs much like our land based wolves, and often attack seals and large fish, including tuna. (*See Chapter 10.*) Killer whales have even been observed preying on great white sharks.

When a pod of Orcas show up in the vicinity of a school of bluefins, the tuna completely shut down their activities. It is as though they become comatose. Actually, they are frightened of the speed and the power, and yes, the voracious appetite they know killer whales possess.

In August of 1979, on a bright, sunny Sunday morning, I was anchored on the SW corner of Stellwagen Bank, along with about 200 other boats, "tuna-wishing." By 0800 hrs, there had been 18 or 20 hook-ups and the bite was still on. There were plenty of inverted V's on my paper recorder and my mate Bruce Hebert and I were expecting to hook-up any minute. (Tuna that cross under a transducer make that inverted V mark on the screen.)

Suddenly, Bruce grabbled my arm and pointed. Cutting cleanly through the water, about a quarter mile to starboard, were two telltale dorsal fins. The distinctive stiff, black, triangular shaped fin with about an 18-inch base, standing three-feet high, is immediately recognizable as belonging to an Orca. We watched as the two fins, looking like mirror images of each other, carved a wide curve that defined the sharp edge of the drop-off that goes quickly from a depth of 90 feet to 200 feet. At the end of this arc, the fins slowly sank, and as quickly as they had appeared, they were gone from sight.

On the surface, things returned to the placid Sunday as if nothing had taken place. Most of the fleet had not seen the visitors and the chumming continued as before. Most of the crews on the boats that had observed the fins returned to chumming shortly after the fins had vanished.

Below the surface, significant changes were taking place. The entire tuna community had noted the presence of the intruders, as quickly as a thunderstorm becomes visible in the storm's lightning. No need to await the thunder. Reacting to fear, the fish seek any protection afforded by their environment. The soft muddy bottom, or their backs against the sheer wall, while others form a tight school until the threat abates.

Whatever reaction, you can be sure their overwhelming fear brought the bite to an abrupt end. No creature, land or sea, has a big appetite when confronted with the threat of death.

Without saying a word, Bruce began cleaning up the cockpit as I started to retrieve the hand-lines we had deployed. There was no need to discuss the situation; the inverted Vs were no longer being imprinted on the sounder's paper. Tuna fishing was over for the day, and even "tuna-wishing" might as well be terminated until the Orcas move on. By the time we were ready to retrieve the anchor and head for the barn, 20 or 30 other boats were doing the same thing.

Bruce took a quick visual inventory of the activity and noted that all of them were crewed by experienced fishermen who knew, as stated in the song, "The Gambler" — "you gotta know when to hold 'em and know when to fold 'em." When killer whales show on the tuna grounds, it is time to fold your hand, cut your losses for the day, and drop out of the game.

Talk to an experienced tuna fisherman about the antics and intelligence displayed by the fish they have become addicted to and you will receive an endless variety of tales, both seen and unseen, some true and some untrue, that confirms the magnificence of these creatures. As you listen to these diverse tales, one single thread should present itself throughout: All skilled tuna men have a strong and abiding respect for *Thunnus thynnus.*

Chapter 6

Enforcement – Towering Tuna Troubles

Enforcement has always been a problem for the fisheries. "Too little, too late" seemed to be the rule of thumb, at least as far as the prevailing perception throughout the tuna industry. There are far too many boats spread over the vast vista of ocean, and too few air and sea vehicles monitoring their activities. The odds of being caught while transferring a fish to another boat at sea (a definite no-no when you are only allowed one fish per day) are so low that even the "honest" fishermen are often tempted. A chance to earn $10 a pound for a fish that dresses out at 600 lbs can put quite a bit of pressure on an honest guy who only wants to trade up to a bigger boat.

"Too little and too late" is the usual conclusion drawn, when enforcement becomes the topic of discussion among tuna men. I do not agree with that assertion. The reverse might have just as much credence; maybe we have *too much, too soon.*

The problem of enforcement stems from the bureaucracy that has evolved since the advent of the Magnuson Fishery Conservation and Management Act (200-mile limit). There are so many levels of government bureaus involved with so many rules, regulations, directive and laws competing for control that they have trouble communicating with each other.

"BUREAUS" must be an acronym for: Big Uncontrollable Regulatory Extravagant And Unnecessary Systems." *(See Chapter 7)*

Federal and State enforcement agencies have the same jurisdictional discrepancies. For instance, the U. S. Coast Guard is a federal agency, yet it has the right to board, apprehend or detain vessels in state waters, even within harbors. (Thankfully, their search and rescue tactics can also be used anywhere their vessel can go.)

In addition to all of their other duties *(mentioned in Chapter 8)*, the CG has also been appointed the task of enforcing all existing fishery laws and regulations. The USCG is not alone. Each state must conform to the federal regulations, but they have the right to change those regulations, as long as those changes are more stringent that the federal minimums. Each state, in order to exercise its own states-rights, has its own bureaus, and of course, its own rules, regulations, directives and laws. All the state bureaus, naturally, spawn their own enforcement forces. It's the domino effect at its most ineffective!

Scenario – Tuna Tangles

A tuna fisherman, with his state and federal tuna permits in hand, leaves his home port of Kennebunkport, Maine, aboard his boat *Bopper*, and proceeds southward in search of bluefin. There is no bite around the Isle of Shoals, so he continues south to search Ipswich Bay, which is also non-productive. The skipper decides to try his luck in Massachusetts's waters, but finds no activity in either Massachusetts Bay or Cape Cod Bay. He proceeds through Cape Cod Canal and works his way south and westward and finally hooks up and boats a tuna in Rhode Island Sound.

Bopper is now three states away from its homeport. Transporting the catch to Kennebunkport is not an option. It is a two-day steam and those 48 hours would mean deterioration and devaluation of his catch. Furthermore, since the fish was taken in Rhode Island waters, technically, it is a RI fish and should be landed in that state. The skipper has no knowledge of the RI state tuna regulations and, since he is relatively close to Martha's Vineyard, he decides to land his fish in Menemsha – a Massachusetts island port with a tuna dealer.

Having previously caught tuna in Ipswich Bay (Massachusetts state waters) and become acquainted with some local tuna fishermen, the skipper feels there is no problem if he takes this fish to a Massachusetts tuna buyer. Wrong!

All vessels landing tuna for sale in any port along the eastern seaboard must have a valid federal tuna permit. (They must also be in compliance with all the federal safety regulations and have all the required USGC approved safety equipment onboard.)

The skipper radios ahead to the fish buyer in Menemsha, informing him of his catch and giving his ETA (Estimated Time of Arrival).

When the buyer boards *Bopper,* he checks the valid federal permit and safety equipment. Ok. Next, he asks to see a Massachusetts Commercial Fishing Permit. *Bopper* doesn't have the required permit. Every boat that is documented or registered in Massachusetts, as well as any boat from anywhere, that intends to sell fish to any fish dealer in the state, must have this permit.

The skipper asks for the quickest way to get a permit. He is told he must go to the Division of Marine Fisheries headquarters in Boston, or call and have an application sent to his home in Maine.

Having run afoul of the Mass. Regulations, the skipper's next inquiry? "Where can I get 500 lbs of ice?" He will need at least that much to ice-down the tuna right away and have a reserve to keep the catch as cold as possible, for at least a day and a half, while he beats his way back to Kennebunkport.

The regulations for selling fish in most other states are very similar to those of Massachusetts – except for the *Bopper's* home state of Maine. Any boat can purchase a permit to sell tuna in a Maine port, at the time of landing, as long as the fishing trip originated from a port outside of Maine. However, if the trip originated from a Maine port, the vessel must have obtained the permit prior to its departure. Go figure!

Confused? Now you have an idea why most fishermen would love to see the regulations, at least those having nothing to do with safety at sea, consolidated and simplified. I have a suspicion that most government officials, at all levels, would welcome laws and regulations that they could at least begin to understand.

State Rights & Wrongs

All the states have spawned organizations, under various names, to oversee the protection of their marine resources. (Maine - Department of Marine Resources, Rhode Island & Connecticut - Department of Environmental Management, Massachusetts - Divison of Marine Fisheries, etc.)

In order to do a thorough job, these organizations should be staffed with marine biologists, environmentalists, legislators and an advisory committee made up of knowledgeable fishermen from both the commercial and recreational sectors. IF the organization is balanced and acting for the good of the resource, our fisheries should be healthy AND sustainable. (That "if" is usually in some doubt. I have yet to see any advisory committee at any level that is *balanced*.)

Of course, any governmental agency that produces regulations (don't they all?) must have some way of enforcing all those regulations. For instance, within the Massachusetts Division of Marine Fisheries, that task falls on the Environmental Police. They have jurisdiction within all state waters, both salt and fresh, and are responsible for enforcing all regulations pertaining to all marine life – shell and fin – and the habitat in which they live.

Towns – Harbormasters

Harbormasters are the chief police officers for the waters that lie within each town's limits. That is a very simple statement of their duties. In most towns, they are also the shellfish officer, the person in charge of moorings, launch facilities, ramps, town floats, and harbor parking for both cars and trailers. They are also responsible for all pump-out facilities, overseeing the general safety of the boating public, and are usually the first to respond to any boating accidents.

Harbormasters must have a working knowledge of all the federal, state and local fishing regulations, and are expected to cooperate fully with all the other enforcement agencies and their personnel. On top of all that, they are town employees, subject to the town government and its officials. That is one hell of a full slate! The position of Harbormaster is one of the most complicated, and possibly under-appreciated town jobs, no matter how large or small its harbor and bay may be.

"What a tangled web we weave..." (Shakespeare)

The enforcement vessels range in size from 500-foot USCG cutters to 21-foot Rigid Inflatable Boats (RIBs) manned by various agency personnel: Federal – USCG and NMFS, State – Environmental and State Police, and Town Harbormasters.

With this broad array of constabulary types, one could imagine the waters to be under constant surveillance, with officers behind every buoy. The opposite is the real truth of the situation. There are two reasons why enforcement is so inadequate: the sea is so vast, and the powers-that-be are woefully undermanned. This is real: Too little and too late.

As a result of all the overlapping of authority and responsibility, enforcement, despite all its visibility, presents a picture that is as hazy as Cape Cod Bay, after a three-day nor'easter.

I remember one incident that happened near the end of the 1970s. An altercation erupted between two boats on the SW corner of Stellwagen Bank. One of the boats hooked a fish on a landline and during the fight; the fish swam under another boat, surfacing on the other side, out of sight of the first boat. The crew of the second boat "ironed" the fish, quickly tail-roped it and got underway to bleed it.

The first boat, hauling in its handline, found it led to the fish being bled by the second boat and a "heated discussion" immediately followed between the crews of the two boats. Fish were bringing $12 to $15 per pound at that time, and of course greed reared its ugly head.

The crew of the second boat proceeded to pick up the fish, placing it in the cockpit, then hauled their anchor and headed for Green Harbor. The first boat began circling the other slower boat, while both crews claimed ownership of the fish with obscene gestures and shouts.

Before the two boats reached port, word had gotten to the Harbormaster and he had alerted the local police about a possible problem that might take place in the public parking lot. The domino effect started. When the two boats arrived, the harbormaster, the local police, state police, and environmental police greeted them. The two crews were still engaged in their ongoing shouting match, while the authorities tried to figure out which branch of enforcement should do the investigating.

The state police were able to separate the two crews and the environmental police began taking statements from members of each crew. The local police were making sure the dispute did not expand into the large crowd that had gathered.

After reviewing the statements of the crewmembers of each of the boats, the investigating officers asked the captains if either wished to prefer charges. Neither one wanted the hassles that would result from preferring charges, not did they want the fish impounded as a consequence.

The next step was to get each crew to agree to abide by the decision of the authorities. The situation was telephoned to the Mass. Division of Marine Fisheries Environmental Police headquarters, where the "final answer" was formulated.

The fish was awarded to the second boat, solely because of the fact it had possession of the fish when it was officially landed.

The International, Federal and State legislators continue to develop new rules, regulations, directives and laws to address each new problem, real or perceived. A new bureau or commission is created to deal with the issue – instead of delegating the job to one of the enforcement bodies that already exists.

The various town, state, federal and international governing bodies, in their attempts to control the tuna fishery so it will remain viable and sustainable, have created a montage of regulations so complicated that even the most astute tuna fishermen shake their heads in disbelief.

As these regulatory bodies continue to stack up, it's no wonder so many tuna fishermen would like to see most of them buried at sea.

Chapter 7

Alphabet Soup has Gotcha

I have always been a believer in the "KISS" principle (Keep It Simple, Stupid). My fascination with acronyms goes way back to the mid-1930s, when President Roosevelt (FDR) began setting up new government agencies to get the US out of the depression. CCC (Civil Conservation Corps); NRA (National Recovery Act... not the present-day National Rifle Association); and WPA (Work Products Administration) are some of the very early acronyms that became "household words."

One of my favorites is the evolution of the word SPUD — for potato. During the famine in Ireland in the mid-1800s, the only food available to the populace was potatoes. In a famine situation, disease is inevitable and an illness that spread throughout the country was attributed to the eating of rotten potatoes. They quickly set up an organization to combat the spread of the disease: SPUD. (**S**ociety for the **P**revention of **U**rinary **D**iseases.)

Federal and state governments over the years seemed to develop a passion for churning out acronyms. That passion, regrettably, will probably never subside.

Fishermen were not really affected by most of them, except for the IRS (Internal Revenue Service) until 1976, when President Gerald Ford signed the 200-mile-limit law. It was dubbed the FCMA (Fishery Conservation and Management Act) in official federal government jargon.

Most fishermen are familiar with the terms LORAN, RADAR and GPS, as "words" that are used in normal everyday dialogue and understood by all. But when it comes to the hundreds of acronyms spawned since President Ford signed that bill, it means that SOURS. (See definitions at the end of this chapter).

Here is a sample excerpt copied from the Federal Register of

October 26, 1998, pertaining to new rules that would affect all tuna, shark, and swordfish fishermen:

"Proposed Rules

"Upon implementation of the HMS FMP, the Secretary will issue Atlantic tunas and North American swordfish regulations under the authority of both the Magnuson-Stevens Act and the ATCA. Regulations issued under the authority of the ATCA carry out the recommendations of the International Commission for the Conservation of Atlantic Tunas (ICCAT).

"The HMS FMP will define overfishing status determination criteria, which designate western Atlantic bluefin tuna, North American swordfish, and large coastal sharks of the Atlantic as overfished. NMFS has developed a domestic rebuilding strategy that identifies biomass and fishing mortality targets, and proposes a suite of management alternatives designed to reduce fishing mortality, bycatch, and bycatch mortality. Preferred alternatives include measures to rebuild overfished fisheries in timeframes consistent with guidelines for implementation of national standard 1 of the Magnuson-Stevens Act, to control fishing effort and allocate domestic landing quotas, and to address issues of safety at sea, enforcement, permitting, reporting, and catch monitoring."

I know it doesn't take a rocket scientist to interpret the Register gobbledygook, but it sure helps if you take the time to read it twice.

The following mythical example of a bull session could occur in any harbor where knowledgeable fishermen discuss the state of their fisheries. How to understand and comply with the often complicated and confusing regulations, and still be able to enjoy the thrill of capturing the sea's most challenging adversary has become a real conundrum.

Doug and Jeff were engaged in a serious gut-wrenching discourse. The latest NMFS regulations had just been released and they were discussing the problems they could see ahead for all tuna fishermen. They were trying to plan a course of action that would let the "powers that be" know just how angry and frustrated the tuna fishermen had become.

Most members of this community had accepted the safety-at-sea provisions and the overall quota designations, but when it comes to the way that quotas is allocated – well, that's when the "shit hits the fan." The regulators are very successful in pitting fisherman against fisherman by trying to split the overall quotas among the various categories (general, harpoon, angler, seiner) and even by location (north or south of Cape Cod).

Doug was in favor of starting at the top with the Secretary of Commerce and working down through the head of NOAA, to NMFS, and the NEFMC, with a shot at the ASMFC and the MAFMC. Jeff injected that they shouldn't overlook the HMS. After all, they came under the ESA, both of which were subject to the EPA. The HMS FMP describes and identifies the EFH of Atlantic tunas.

Doug continued his line of thinking, "even though we catch tuna in the EEZ, we can't bypass the DMF, DMR,F&W, or the two DEMs, because that's where our catches will be landed. We have to remember both the MSFCMA and the ATCA carry out the recommendations of ICCAT, which can do nothing to slow down the catch rate of those nations that are not members of ICCAT." Doug's voice wavered for a second. Then he asked Jeff what he thought.

Jeff thought Doug's approach was okay, but he wanted to make sure we DUMB! Jeff's idea was to start from the other end, with the grass-roots. He proposed they start with the fishermen's organizations – the ECTA,GCTA, HCTA, NSCTA and the CCCHFA. Maybe even include the seiners. "Try to get them all working for the same goals." (Really, Jeff…Is that possible? Not!) He wanted them to work out and agree on a "fishermen's" FMP and submit it to DFM, DMR, F&W, and the two DEMs. "If those state organizations could come to a consensus of opinion, then submit the FMP to the NEFMC, it would put pressure on them to lean on NMFS, which would relay the concerns to NOAA, and eventually get to the SOC."

Jeff paused for a second, furrowed his brow, then continued. "Of course, the FMC would have to take into account the revised MSFCMA, ATCA and SFA, and the draft HMS FMP, all of which are subject to the EPA."

At this point, Doug interjected another thought to add to the soup-d'jour. "At lease we seem to be making progress along scientific lines with the advent of the SCRS and the ACCSP. Maybe they will be a big help in the ICCAT, NMFS, ASMFC and MAFMC deliberations."

Jeff ended the conversation with, "We should never ignore the many existing conservation organizations, such as the WWF, SPC, CMC, NCMC, CCA, and of course the umbrella of them all under the RFA. We should hold out hope that the SCRS and the ACCSP results can help both the tuna and the tuna fishermen!"

If you are confused by the above dialogue, you are definitely not alone! In fact you are in the majority. Even the members of the various commissions have a "list-of-terms" at hand for quick reference. I sometimes think it's a matter of GOTCHA... (Government Organizations Think Citizen Harassment is Acceptable) I call this my own GOTCHA, which is just another acrimonious acronym that could also stand for Glossary Of Terms Can Help Acronyms)

Federal Departments & Agencies (from the top down)
SOC – Secretary of Commerce
NOAA – National Oceanic and Atmospheric Administration
NMFS – National Marine Fisheries Service
ASMFC – Atlantic States Marine Fisheries Commission
MAFMC – Mid-Atlantic Fisheries Management Council

Government Groups Under NMFS
SCRS – Standing Committee on Research and Science
ACCSP – Atlantic Coastal Cooperative Statistics Program

Federal Acts (having impact on tuna fisheries)
MSFCMA – Magnuson-Stevens Fishery Conservation and Management Act
FCMA – (same as above, without the sponsors names)
ATCA – Atlantic Tunas Conservation Act
SFA – Sustainable Fisheries Act
HMS – Highly Migratory Species
EPA – Environmental Protection Act/Agency
EEC – Exclusive Economic Zone
SBNMS – Stellwagen Bank National Marine Sanctuary

State Organizations (of the Five New England Coastal States)
DMF – Division of Marine Fisheries (Massachusetts)
DMR – Department of Marine Resources (Maine)
FAW – Fish and Wildlife (New Hampshire)
DEM – Department of Environmental Management (Rhode Island and Connecticut)
Conservation Organizations
WWF – World Wildlife Fund
SPC – Sea Party Coalition
CMC – Center for Marine Conservation
NCMC – National Coalition for Marine Conservation
CCA – Coastal Conservation Association
RFA – Recreational Fishing Alliance

Fisherman's Organizations
ECTA – East Coast Tuna Association
GCTA – General Category Tuna Association
HCTA – Harpoon Category Tuna Association
NSCTA – North Shore Community Tuna Association
CCCHFA – Cape Cod Commerical Hook Fishermen's Association

Common Marine Acronyms
RADAR – RAdio Detection And Range
LORAN – LOng Range Aids to Navigation
SONAR – SOund Navigation And Range (underwater)

GPS – Global Positioning System
DGPS – Differential Global Positioning System

Old, New and Some Fictitious Acronyms

BUREAUS – Big Uncontrollable Regulatory Extravagant and Unnecessary Systems
KISS – Keep It Simple, Stupid
DUMB – Don't Underestimate Marine Biologists
GRUB – Get Relief in Understanding Bureaucracy
NOT – Never Obviously Together
SOURS – Sometimes Our Understanding Really Sucks!
FLOOD – Front Line Of Our Defense

If this chapter helps you GRUB and you find your way through the government gobbledygook, that is the good news. The bad news is, all of the above has only to do with the tuna fishery… wait till you weigh in on the bottom fish, sport fish, shellfish, mammals, and the rest of the HMS, each of which has its own complete set of acronyms.

I am willing to bet that by the time you read this, the combinations of the International, Federal, State And Local Administrative Dogma (IF-SALAD) forces will have come up with at least double-digit, new and exciting (?) ways to make it more difficult for us to GRUB.

Don't forget… it's not your fault if SOURS! The government agencies are NOT, so if you want to GRUB, put the blame on the bureaucrats, write letters to your Senators and Representatives telling them to KISS, and make sure they DUMB… after all, when it comes to tuna stocks, they are the FLOOD.

Bottom line…. If you havn't yet let the GOTCHA getcha, I'll betcha sooner or later it's gon'a ketcha!!!!!!!

Chapter 8

The Fish & The Safety Inspection

"Looks like we're next on the list. We'd better get the safety equipment ready for inspection." Ray and I had been watching the progress of the Coast Guard inspection team as they worked their way north along the thin line of boats that were anchored in 120 feet of water along the steep drop-off that forms the north-west corner of Stellwagen Bank. All the boats had their lines set out and they were chumming heavily, hoping to hook-up to a bluefin tuna.

"You're right. They seem to be boarding every other boat, and only the *Stinger* lies between us and the *White Out*, which is going to be their next victim." I went below to get out the *Misty* documents I knew they would be requesting to see. Ray busied himself opening the life jacket storage spaces.

God bless the Coast Guard. They are charged with maintaining all the aids to navigation, interdiction of the flow of drugs, protection of our coastlines and harbors, enforcement of the international and national laws of the sea, and assuring the safety and well-being of the commercial and recreational fleets, etc., etc., etc. These dedicated men and women also endeavor to keep the public educated about all these many matters for which they are responsible.

Some fishermen think of the Coast Guard's safety inspections as an imposition. I would disagree completely. Just the fact that they spot-check for safety increases the likelihood that boaters will check their own gear, even if only at the beginning of each season. If you are issued a citation after an inspection, you are forced to correct a problem that might have otherwise caused property damage or loss of life or limb, if allowed to remain neglected. The half-hour you give up for an inspection might keep you and your boat out of the accident statistics.

As we watched the boarding party approach the *White Out*, the crew of the *Stinger*, with their middle fingers erect, yelled to us that we were next on the shit list. My crew and I returned the gesture, and then continued with our chumming chores.

I turned my gaze to the north and noticed the boat next to us looked very relaxed, and the one beyond that was already preparing for their inspection. I imagined this alternating relief-and-sweat mentality would go on until the CG had finished their day's assignment.

I asked Ray to do anything else he could think of to make it easy for the inspection team to complete their job as quickly as possible; after all, we didn't want to lose any more valuable fishing time than necessary.

Ray went below, and reappeared with his arms loaded with life jackets, the ship's bell and cooler. Then he placed the documents and papers on the chum-board.

"They will probably want to look at the engine compartment. It might be better to put the PDFs on the deck, behind the fighting chair," I said as I checked to see f the running lights and anchor light were operating properly. The crew moved the jackets while Ray went below for the third time, and got the spare fire extinguisher and nestled it in the bucket harness on the seat of the fighting chair.

As the CG team was passing the *Stinger*, I looked to the south and made a mental note to commend the *Stinger*'s skipper on the unseemly levity he and his crew had directed at us while the inspection team was boarding the *White Out*.

When the CG Zodiac was about 50 feet off our starboard quarter, the boatswain's mate cupped his hands and hollered, "Permission to come aboard, Sir?" "Permission granted, and welcome," I replied.

As the team slowed to idle speed and made its final approach, the reel of the rod set in the port-stern rod-holder began clicking as the line peeled overboard. "We're hooked up!" Ray yelled as he pulled the rod from the holder, tightened the drag and set the hook. I looked at the Coast Guardsmen and mumbled something about this not being the most convenient time for a safety inspection. He broke into a broad grim and said, "I agree, Captain. Good Luck!" He turned the Zodiac away from us and headed straight for the "relaxed" boat anchored just to our north.

Absolute pandemonium reigned for the next two or three minutes. Ray, Pete (the angler), and his buddy, Sam not only had to deal with the usual hook-up confusion, but this time they were wading in PFDs, fire extinguishers, licenses, ship's papers, the ship's bell and all the rest of the safety gear we'd made ready for the inspection. Sam and Pete were charged with stowing all this gear, along with rods, reels, leaders and hooks, just forward of the engine box. When I looked, I saw that it had all ended up as one very large tangled mound, and during the melee, the chum box had been tipped over and the cockpit was now covered with half-thawed herring.

Somehow, we got underway and settled into the fighting mode. As the fish headed off the edge, into deep water, I had a chance to look back at the Zodiac. As it approached the now "relaxed" boat to the north, I imagined the domino effect taking place as each boat had to reassess its place in the inspection lineup. Those that had formerly been the "by-catch" suddenly had become the "targeted species." I started to smile and then realized I would probably be blamed for their change of fortune.

Ray called out, "The fish is tail-wrapped and is going straight down. Take her out of gear, Cap." I reacted and let the fish tow us toward a dragger that was anchored 100 yard to the west. The steep angle of the line made our forward progress rather slow and at the same time put additional strain on the fish. I was starting to bring the bow around so I would be able to walk the fish aft of the dragger, when Ray said the fish had just suddenly stopped swimming.

These creatures never stop the fight until they are dead. I

maneuvered *Misty* to the point where the line was straight up and down, which put us only a few feet from the starboard quarter of the dragger.

The skipper of the dragger looked down into the cockpit and asked if there was anything he could do to assist us. "No thanks, Cap, it's our problem. We think the fish must have suffered an aneurysm and buried his head in the mud. You might take up on your anchor line a bit to move us apart and give us some maneuvering room. We're going to try to cut him out of the mud."

As one of his crew started forward to comply, there was a telltale breaker string "snap" from the dragger's port side. Instead of taking up on their anchor line his crewmember merely pulled the quick release and the dragger moved off with its own hook-up. I glanced at Ray and said, "I really don't think the skipper had to go that far to give us some room."

I put the wheel hard over and slipped *Misty* into idle while Ray explained to Pete that we were going to try to cut the suction around the fish with the line, by making circles. Ray tightened the drag to the point of breaking strength and had Pete hold the rod at a 45-degree angle for maximum lifting pressure.

After three or four circles, there was a little give in the rod. I put the rudder amid-ship and headed for the deeper water. We were able to pull the fish free of the muck. I took *Misty* out of gear and, with the line slowly leaving the spool, we all watched as the fish settled to the bottom again. "I don't want to tighten the drag anymore. We're already putting too much stress on the line. Guess we're going to have to hand-line this one."

Ray went into the cabin to get some rags for our hands. The agreed procedure was for Pete to take up the line as steady as possible, never lowering the rod-tip, so as to avoid any start-stop, start-stop motion that would create extra pressure on the line. Ray and I were to alternate hands, with one of us on each side of the rod. Once we had the fish started, there was to be no pause until we had him at the transom. Sam was to have the tail rope at the ready as soon as the fish broke the surface.

For the next 45 minutes there was total concentration and total silence on board, except for the grunts and groans of the angler, the captain and Ray, the majority of which came from the captain.

What little breeze there had been that morning had dropped off and the bright sun was pushing the thermometer well into the 90s. It had only taken a few minutes for Ray, Pete and I to become soaked in our own sweat. Halfway into the struggle, I began to envy Sam his duty as the tail-roper.

I had appointed Ray and myself as the DHs (which in this league stood for Designated Haulers) because we were the only ones on board who had experience with handling tuna. Somehow, we were able to establish a steady rhythm as we slowly winched the prey toward the surface being careful to never slow down or stop our "hauler."

When we reached the double line, I told Sam to stand by to tail-rope. When the swivel came into sight, we noticed the leader was wrapped around both tailfin lobes and had almost severed one of them. When the tail broke the surface, Sam dropped the loop over it and cinched it up tight. A cheer, more of relief and exhaustion than joy, broke out while Sam cleated off the tail rope, saying "That wasn't so tough, was it?" If anyone aboard had had any strength left, Sam would have taken a swim.

Besides having been brought up tail first as a dead weight, there were several other things that made this fish unique. Both of its gill plates were wide open and full of bottom ooze, giving us an indication of just how far it had penetrated into the mud. All of its dorsal and anal finlets, normally a bright yellow, were a brilliant vermilion. This is almost always an indication that the fish has died from an aneurysm. It is very possible this was brought on by the fish's struggle to tow the boat at such a very steep angle.

Normally, a tail-wrapped fish will have at least one of its gills held closed by the leader. In this case, the leader came from the corner of the jaw, straight aft across the belly meat and around the bottom lobe of the tail and over the top lobe. The leader had cut the bottom lobe near the caudal keel, from the rear to as far as the bony leading edge.

We raked the gills and towed the fish backwards until the mud washed out and the fish was bled.

As we were returning to our anchor ball, I noticed the Coast Guard boarding party was still working its way north along the thin line of boats, still anchored along the sharp drop-off.

Suddenly, the VHF radio barked, "Hey, *Misty*. I guess you know half the boats in the fleet think you're a Jonah for changing the pattern of the 'rubber-ducky' inspection team." Almost immediately another voice, "Yeah, you got a new name now — Captain Jonah, — thanks for nothing." There was a short silence and then a third voice, "You could screw up a one-car funeral!" I recognized all three of the voices as those belonging to captains of boats from my own harbor.

Some genuine friends, green with envy, who couldn't wait to "twist the knife" when one of their buddies was getting ready to return to the harbor with the only fish taken so far that day.

I waited a few seconds and then keyed my mike, "Let's look at it this way ... the other half of the boats must think I brought about a blessing-of-the-fleet."

Chapter 9

Dr. Daniel: Dangerous Dingbat

I watched the charter personnel start down the ramp and I knew right away that we were not going to have any trouble when we hooked-up. All four members were over six feet tall and looked as if they were models for Calvin Klein, or maybe fresh out of Gold's Gym. This was a tuna handline charter, and for once, I knew the "crew" would not "leave the hauling to us."

The last few days had seen a drop in the number of fish being hooked on the SW corner of Stellwagen Bank, so Bruce, the mate, and I had decided to fish the NW corner, for a change of venue.

We dropped anchor in 120 feet of water, near the steep drop off on the western most point of the corner. The current was flowing in a westerly direction, which swung us over the steep slope.

Bruce paid out 300 feet of rode, and when *Misty* came taut on the anchor she had only 175 feet under her keel. I told Bruce to let out another 100 feet of line, which would place *Misty* over the bottom of the slope in our favorite depth of 250 feet.

Bruce set out our anchor ball and came aft to start the chum slick, while I set up a quick-release line.

I checked our position and noted that the nearest boat was a 20-foot Mako, center console, with only one person aboard. *Misty* settled about 50 yards south of the Mako, a distance that gave plenty of room to maneuver, even if both of us hooked-up at the same time.

The tide was one hour from dead low, and we hadn't yet seen any activity anywhere in the fleet. I told the Calvin-Klein-crew that things often pick up after the change of the tide. All we needed do was to keep the slick going until the fish were ready to eat.

At dead low, the current slackened and a breeze sprang up from the SW, pushing *Misty* slowly to the northeastward into shallower water toward the top of the slope. I noticed we were moving closer to the Mako. The extra 100 feet of anchor line we had deployed was allowing us to scribe a bigger arc than the Mako, as both boats swung around to the north. I was hoping the distance between the two boats would not get too short and result in us having to haul anchor and move to a much less desirable spot.

Bruce asked if I thought the skipper of the Mako was the notorious "Doctor Daniel". I glanced at the skipper again, and told Bruce I didn't have the foggiest.

The "doctor" in question was not a doctor of medicine, but a man with a PhD in physics. The stories circulating through the tuna fleet about Dr. Daniel's history were definitely different than those of any other tuna fisherman. I heard he'd worked his way through Massachusetts Institute of Technology, receiving a masters degree in just three years, and then went on to earn his PhD from Harvard University, one of the youngest to ever receive a doctorate from that prestigious institution. Rumor had it that all this academic pressure on the very young, highly intelligent man was just too much for him, and he became a system dropout at the age of 23, having never applied any of the training and knowledge he'd gained.

When he surfaced in the tuna fishery, he had become fascinated with the physical nature of a one-on-one battle with a bluefin. He purchased a Mako and began developing his own technique for handlining giants. He avoided all social contact – always fishing alone. Dr. Daniel soon earned a reputation as a highliner often having a streak of 6 or 7 fish in a row – and always being careful not to disclose any of the "secrets" he had developed on his own. He was also known to have a volatile temper that often exploded for reasons known only to him.

One explosion occurred when he brought in a fish that dressed out at over 500 pounds. The dealer offered him the going price for that day, the same price the dealer had just given to other fishermen. However, Dr. Daniel demanded another 50¢ a pound, saying that his fish was of a superior quality. When the dealer insisted the offer was as high as he could go. Dr. Daniel went into one of his tantrums, had the fish put into the Mako, and steamed out of the harbor. Observers said the Doctor was back getting bait for the next day's fishing within 45 minutes. The bait dealer said there had been no evidence of the 500-pound tuna ever being aboard the Doctor's Mako, and since the nearest tuna buyer was more than an hour away ... everyone wondered what happened to the Doctor's catch. (The going price for tuna that day was $4.50 per pound, making a fish of that size worth $2,250.)

The current began to pick up from windward, pushing us even further up the slope and closing the gap between *Misty* and the Mako. We had arrived after the Mako, so it was up to us to move if we drifted too close. I noticed the Mako's skipper moving around the center console, kicking the hull as he went, and staring at *Misty*. I concurred with Bruce that the skipper must be Dr. Daniel. After all, only whackos would kick their own Makos.

The gap had closed to about 25 yards when Dr. Daniel exploded and began shouting invectives worthy of a four-hitch Navy veteran. Of course, every other word began with an F, and everyone aboard *Misty* was labeled an "asshole".

When he ran out of breath, I was finally able to tell him we were just about to haul anchor when he exploded, but now I didn't give a damn who was here first. This brought on more screaming, more kicking, more invectives, and threats, all of which were ignored by captain and crew.

The distance between the boats continued to close and suddenly there was quiet. Dr. Daniel began walking in circles around his console. This time there was no kicking or yelling.

His head was down, his flushed face gradually fading to a deathly gray. His eyes were moist and his hands were gesturing as though he were discussing some internal conflict that only he could resolve.

His mostly unintelligible mumbling was interjected with some discernable phrases, "...haven't had a fish in seven days; can't get a bite; too many people; this bastard is too close; got to stop him."

Suddenly, his face flushed again and the rage returned. He picked up his cockpit harpoon and, blaming all his problems on *Misty* and her crew, spewed forth a string of contemptuous remarks, interspersed with foul language. He raised the cockpit harpoon, cocked his arm, took aim directly at me and screamed, "I'm going to buttonhole you, you fuckin' son-of-a-bitch!"

With that frightening threat, one of my crew members yelled, "Let's board the bastard, Capt." That's all it took. Dr. Daniel quickly assessed his position in the situation. Un-cocking the harpoon, he lowered his head, went to his knees and seemingly melted into the cockpit sole. The red rage drained from his face, fading to the deathly gray again. He began mumbling again. This time the words were directed entirely within his own psyche.

The crew and I watched this transformation and then I turned the key in the ignition and quietly told Bruce to haul anchor. *Misty* moved away from the Mako at idle speed, leaving Dr. Daniel to his own deranged thoughts.

The member of the crew who had urged us to board the Mako had the last word, "I feel sorry for him; hope he gets help. He's just too pathetic."

.... Seven years later ....

Misty was again tuna "wishing" on the north west corner of Stellwagen Bank. It was afternoon and we had not seen any hook-ups for four hours. I began remembering my confrontation with Dr. Dan and what I had heard about him over the last seven years.

The word among tuna men was that Dr. Dan had straightened out and was once again a highliner. Some who knew him best said he had become adjusted to the life of a fisherman, and had even taken on a mate. I was glad to hear he had made adjustments, but there was no way I was going to believe this antisocial being could ever interact with another human while confined to a boat for a day of fishing!

I had not seen Dr. Dan since the day he had threatened to buttonhole me, and as far as I was concerned, I didn't care if our paths ever crossed again. One other thing I'd heard was that he'd changed boats and now owned a 24-foot Parker with a cuddy cabin.

The bite had come to a complete stop. Most of the boats were chumming heavily just to use up their chum so they could head for home. The charter and I were in a funk and I was ready to turn the fishing trip into a whale-watch. The mate and I had observed only one hook-up – a 24′ Parker – and that fish had taken the boat some two nautical miles eastward to the shallower water well east of the corner. At the time, I had made no connection between the Parker and Dr. Dan.

Kenny, my new mate, dumped what was left of the chum soup over the side and began making "let's go home noises." It was well after high noon.

Since we had had no luck at all with the fishing, I suggested to the crew that we go see some whales. They agreed; anything was better than doing nothing.

While Kenny hauled the anchor, I remembered the one hook-up of the day, now almost four hours ago. I scanned the waters to the east and spotted the Parker. Its attitude seemed to suggest it was still working the fish. I told the crew, "On the way to the whale feeding grounds, we'll check out the boat with the only hook-up of the day, and maybe they will get an up-close look at the species we were unable to put a hook into." Curiosity also played a big part in my decision. I had to find out if it was Dr. Dan, and if so, why it was taking him so long to boat the fish.

On our way Kenny was in his glory as he told the crew the story of the altercation his older brother, Bruce, and I had had with Dr. Dan, seven years ago. He ended his somewhat enhanced tale by saying that he didn't think this could possibly be *that* Dr. Dan, because *that* Dr. Dan had built a reputation on the fact that he rarely took more than 20 minutes to bring his hand lined tuna to the tail rope.

At a distance of one-quarter mile, I dropped to idle speed, focused the binoculars on the Parker and immediately recognized Dr. Dan. Older, scruffier, unshaven, and still with those intensely intelligent, piercing eyes, he was totally immersed in the task at hand. I leaned over the bridge railing and looked at the mate, "Kenny, it's him!"

Dr. Dan and his mate were bent over the gunwale, each holding a line of Sampson cord with both hands, obviously in a struggle to control a bluefin that was making tight circles under the boat.

(The two lines meant that Dr. Dan had had the fish close enough to add a dart line to the hook-up line at some point in the fight.) I dropped into neutral and *Misty* slowly closed the distance.

Dr. Dan became aware of our presence, looked up and a momentary flash of anger emanated from his eyes. I was expecting another explosion. It never came. Our eyes met and his stare seemed to look right through me. A glimpse of recognition showed for a split second, but the thought was followed instantly by a blink of rejection.

A sardonic smile played on his lips as he calmly explained that this was the toughest f'n fish he'd ever f'n hooked, and he and his mate had been fighting this f'n fish for f'n four f'n hours, and he would appreciate it if we would f'n back f'n off till they had the f'n fish f'n tail roped.

I was glad he had at least narrowed his four-hitch Navy language down to one f'n four-letter word.

I put *Misty* in reverse and backed away until I had 20 yards of water between the two boats. I shut down the engine so the crew, Kenny, and I could watch and listen.

Dr. Dan and his mate struggled together, alternately lifting and holding, with a turn over the gunwale, until the fish was hauled to the surface. The fish was thrashing and beating its tail against the hull, making a sound much the same as the sound Dr. Dan had produced seven years before, when he was kicking the inside hull of his Mako.

Dr. Dan passed his dart line to the mate and told him to "take a turn over the gunwale with both f'n lines and f'n hold the f'n fish right there." Then he disappeared into the cabin.

When he emerged, he had an "Oozie" in one hand and a spare clip in the other. He very calmly emptied the first clip into the right side of the fish's head, reloaded, moved to the other side of the mate and fired the second clip. He raised the Oozie overhead, waved in triumph and shouted, "I finally f'n got him!"

Kenny expressed everyone's thoughts in one succinct sentence, "Let's get the hell out of here! He's still nuts!"

.... Three years later ....

I was attending a National Marine Fisheries Service public hearing that was being held to get input from tuna fishermen about some new regulations that were being proposed for the next season.

I noticed a distinguished looking gentleman sitting near the front of the hall. He was wearing a suit and had a briefcase on the floor, under his seat. He could never be taken for a fisherman. The rest of the audience was in dungarees and pullovers. There was something familiar about his looks, but I just couldn't place him.

The meeting started out with the familiar harangues and partisan statements from fishermen representing the various categories; each trying to make a point for their particular interests. When the meeting was about to turn into a shouting match, the chairman called for order. When there was some semblance of a return to civility, the chair recognized the gentleman seated near the front.

As he picked up his brief case and approached the microphone, I was able to get a better view, and recollection suddenly came into focus. Dr. Daniel! He was clean-shaven with a recent hair cut, looking distinguished, educated, and ... sane.

Dr. Dan opened a folder he had taken from his brief case and delivered a learned talk on the plight of the Atlantic Bluefin Tuna, and offered his opinion of what should be done, both federally and internationally, to insure a healthy and sustainable fishery. He had back-up facts, which were presented in a clearly understandable and convincing way. The audience was quiet and attentive.

The remarkable thing about this presentation was that it addressed all the tuna problems: biologically, politically and economically. It contained ideas that might simplify the regulatory morass the fishery had become. Above all, it was stated in a way that made sense to everyone in attendance.

When he ended his speech, he presented his notes to the chair and walked out of the hall to the prolonged applause from the fishermen.

It was the mid-80s then, and I have not seen or heard of Dr. Daniel since.

Chapter 10

Orca Orgy in P'town Harbor

Most orca are nothing like Shamu or Willie as portrayed in Sea World or the dizzy world of Disney. Vacationers who visit the various Sea Worlds see these creatures as cute, personable, intelligent and entertaining. Enchanted viewers watch the trained orca being lead through benign routines, jumping through hoops, retrieving objects from the bottom of the pool, giving bare-back rides to their handlers, and generally doing the same things we have come to expect from their dolphin counterparts — only in a much larger and more spectacular manner.

Seeing these antics, I realize they are the products of rigorous and expert training, patterned after dog training methods. Each time an orca completes a task successfully, it is rewarded with a handful of food. I'll bet that most of the trainers are part "Pavlov" and that most mammals would give up their day job if they were assured of being fed regularly just for "jumping through hoops." Yes, BUT … (and this is a very capital BUT) their true persona is actually much closer to that of their other name: Killer Whale.

As noted at the end of Chapter 5, just the presence of these killer whales in the vicinity of a tuna fleet can shut down the fishing until the tuna know the coast is clear. Killer whales are one of the world's largest and most powerful mammals. Their size (up to 25 feet long) and weight (several tons) would seem to inhibit their mobility. Wrong! They can move that length and weight at upwards of 35 knots with the agility of the Atlantic Mackerel.

There is a National Geographic Society video about orca which captures an attack on mature seals. Orcas grab ar the seals violently, instantly breaking their necks, ther into the air (completely clear of the water) as they rush on to attack another seal. That gruesome vision gives the viewer a good idea of the orca's strength, speed and agility — and a fair hint of their predatory persona. It also illustrates a feeding-frenzy of major proportions.

Almost every serious fisherman has seen bluefish or striped bass feeding-frenzies suddenly erupt. Occasionally, other species display this behavior also. There are even frenzies involving spiny dogfish feeding on the surface. During these occurrences, it doesn't matter what lures are thrown into the frenzy – the fisherman is going to hook-up.

A frenzy is most often triggered by animals that are classified as predators: on land, it is wolves, jackals, coyotes and the like; in the air, it is the falcons, hawks and even owls; and in the sea, it's bluefish, fluke, wolf fish and most sharks. There are many more predators throughout the world, but when it comes right down to it, mankind is the supreme predator of all the species. Some predators, especially wolves, have been observed working together in a cooperative way for the good of the whole pack. Even non-predator members of the animal world sometimes engage in feeding frenzies, as a result of extreme hunger.

When a true land or water-based predator's feeding-frenzy gets out of hand, it escalates to the next level, and becomes a killing-frenzy. At this higher level, food is no longer the object. The participants are now killing purely for the thrill of the kill!

Orca may not be portrayed as predators in the "Wonderful World of Disney," but the incident that occurred in Provincetown Harbor, Mass. in July of 1974, revealed a much darker side of our real "Wonderful World."

The outer harbor of P'town has a depth of 30 feet or more for two nautical miles measuring west to east, and one nautical mile south to north from the #3 buoy at its entrance. Shallows consisting of hard sand to the east, and mud flats to the westward border the perimeter of this two-mile rectangle. The entrance channel has an average width of 100 feet. This well-protected anchorage is large enough to anchor the entire Atlantic Fleet of the U.S. Navy.

Early one morning in mid-July, a pack of killer whales (exactly how many is unknown) herded a large school of bluefin tuna into the confines of the P'town Harbor; and for the better part of that day, the orca kept them balled-up and the bluefin were in a frantic and irrational state, unable to gain their freedom.

Eyewitnesses reported seeing orca swimming back and forth across the entrance to the harbor, seemingly on patrol, to discourage any attempted escapes. Others reported seeing the orca circling the captives, much like bluefish will constantly circle baitfish to keep them "corralled" and controlled.

When in a feeding-frenzy, bluefish will ravage the weaker members of the school that are unable to power their way into the safety at the center of the "ball." Feeding on the "easy-pickin's" might be the trigger that turns frenzy from feeding to killing.

Some reports of this day's carnage stated the killer whales attacked, killed, and then immediately turned and sought another victim. Hunger did not seem to be the reason for the slaughter. As the day wore on, it became more and more evident that the feeding had turned to killing. I interviewed one reliable source that saw no feeding at all, only killing. "Those damn whales were killing just for the fun of it," he told me.

Master fisherman Manny Phillips (see Chapter 12) reported seeing a killer whale clear the surface of the water with an estimated 500-pound tuna in its mouth. (And, believe me, if anyone could estimate the weight of a tuna, it was Captain Manny!) Here was one example of the raw power of an orca, able to lift a quarter ton of the ocean's most powerful fish clear of the water, with ease. Disney and Sea World fans forgive me, but I just cannot picture orca as "cute or personable or entertaining" ... except for the macabre-thrill-seeker.

When tuna die, unlike most other fish with large swim-bladders, they don't float belly-up to become food for the birds — they sink to the bottom and become food for a myriad of sea creatures, from the microscopic to grubs, to crustaceans and finfish. Therefore, after the several hours of that day's killing, the two square miles of P'town Harbor must have been carpeted with literally hundreds of dead bluefin.

A mature bluefin will lose over four gallons of blood when bled by the only other predator capable of catching and killing them (Homo sapiens.) By a conservative estimate, some 300 tuna were killed that day. Multiply that by four gallons each, it would equal the amount of blood collected by the Red Cross, at a pint per person, from 9,600 donors!

Twelve hundred gallons of blood can turn a harbor's waters from a beautiful clear blue to an ugly murky brown. One fact of this event stands out very clearly: the amount of blood spilled into the water must have been substantial, because it took two full ten-foot tidal flows (over 24 hours) to flush the harbor and remove the evidence of that monumental blood bath.

Eyewitness accounts confirm that the events of that day were far more than just a feeding-frenzy. It had obviously turned into a killing frenzy. I have often wondered if the orca, at the top of the sea-creature evolution, regret their participation in the carnage of that day, as much as humans, at the top of the land-creature evolution; must regret their actions on the killing fields of Cambodia?

Chapter 11

The Whale & The Tournament

It was the last day of the Green Harbor Tuna Tournament of 1978. The crew of *Misty* was feeling their oats. Allen Frye, a gentleman from Philly, had booked *Misty* for the three-day competition, and we were now in the lead with an 812-pound beauty that Allen's 15-year-old son had angled on the first day.

Two fish had been taken on the second day, but neither was in contention. There had been no hook-ups on this third and final day, and all fishing was to cease at 1600 hours.

We were anchored at the north end of the fleet and had not seen any activity on any of the boats near us. I was standing at the transom, casually chumming, while my real attention was directed toward observing a humpback whale, waving one of his pectoral fins at us. He was about 100 feet off the port quarter, seemingly enjoying the afternoon sun.

Some of my best days of tuna fishing have had nothing to do with tuna. These are the days when it's not your turn to have a hook-up, but it could turn out to be a day that you will remember vividly because of other events. I was getting the feeling that this day was turning into one of those days.

It was pleasantly warm, just right for daydreaming. I remembered one such day when those of us in the fleet witnessed an event that may never take place again. A 100-foot blue whale, the largest mammal ever to live on the planet Earth, came cruising slowly and quietly through the SW corner of Stellwagen Bank as if he had dominion over all he surveyed (at 100-feet and 100-metric tons, he surely had that right!). This is one of those images that will remain in my mind as vividly as though it happened only yesterday. I can still see the dense aqua color that was the result of his azure-blue body blending with the blue of the sea.

Another still-photo etched in my memory took place on one of those dog days of August, when there is no breeze and the temperature is hovering around the mid-90s. There were about 100 boats in the fleet and there hadn't been a single hook-up all morning. The sea was as flat as the proverbial pool table. The calm was so pervasive that you could hear normal conversations from boats 100-yards away.

Ray, the mate, had just made a comment about the sun being at "twelve-o'clock high" when there was a rush of sound to our port. We both spun around in that direction just in time to see a 45-foot humpback whale suspended six-feet above the surface of the water, in an open space between the boats! The resulting splash, as his 40-ton body pancaked on the surface, created three-foot ripples that radiated out from the area of re-entry. As each ripple reached each succeeding boat, there was a momentary rocking; and then, after a full 15-minutes, the calm returned and everyone went back to chumming.

My reminiscing ended abruptly when the nearby humpback decided to get our attention, and slapped the water with his 30-foot pectoral fin. Then, rolling on his back, he waved both pectorals. We applauded his performance and when he was sure he had won an Oscar, he seemed to tire of showing off and slowly slipped beneath the surface with a final flip of his fluke.

When he surfaced again, he was between *Misty's* transom and our nearest balloon-float. When his right pectoral had passed the balloon, it began to move and the line started slowly peeling off the reel. The crew went into its hook-up drill as Allen picked up the rod, and without setting the hook, sat in the chair and eased off on the drag. When *Misty* had cleared our anchor ball, I spun the boat around and headed her toward the whale. At first we were gaining some line, but that soon changed as the whale went into overdrive. Allen could feel the rod beginning to pulsate. "I think he's got himself tail-wrapped, Cap."

For the next several minutes, everything remained in balance. The humpback and *Misty* seemed to be going at the same pace. Allen looked up at the bridge with a "what do we do now?" expression on his face, and an amused twinkle in his eye.

I had been thinking of alternatives that would not disturb Mr. Humpback, and quickly rejected them all as possibly being detrimental to the whale. Not wanting to do anything to excite our new friend, I decided to put the ball in his court. "Let the drag completely off and I'll take her out of gear. Let's find out what HE has in mind."

As the momentum slowed, our friend began to surface, about 300-yards to our north. The humpback was broadside to *Misty* as we watched in awe as the huge body emerged from the water to a point where it seemed more than half of the whale was above the surface. It was also completely stationary. I took *Misty* out of gear and drifted slowly toward the whale. With a football-field's distance between us, I cut the engine. The only sound was the soft "click" of the dog inside the reel as Allen slowly took-up the slack, without bringing it taught.

No one on board spoke or made a sound. *Misty* came to a complete stop approximately 200 feet from our fascinating friend. As we all stared at this 45-foot beauty, it calmly made eyeball-to-eyeball contact, and then, as if having decided that we were no threat and were members of an inferior species, it lifted its tail almost to vertical, and with one mighty burst of energy, slapped the surface. The sound was much like the crack of a nearby rifle, and the resulting geyser reminded me of those that appear aft of the fantail of a destroyer, made by exploding depth-charges during anti-submarine maneuvers.

When the fluke smashed the water, Allen felt a momentary tug on the rod-tip, and then nothing. Our friend moved off and slid below the surface. Allen began to retrieve the loose line onto the reel, and when the bitter end reached the spool, we could see traces of black felt marker stains on the last two or three feet. Ray always used a black magic-marker to darken all of the double line and for several feet above the Bimini-twist. Allen had retrieved the entire running line, except for 40 feet of double line and a 15-foot leader. The energetic slap had parted the line some 45 feet above the hook.

Given the fact that our friend had been tail-wrapped, we came to the conclusion that the humpback had indeed been hooked when its pectoral fin became ensnared with the leader. The distance from the hook being hooked by the pectoral fin and then leading down to and being wrapped around the tail fin would account for the break being just above the Bimini-twist.

After returning to our anchor ball, I glanced at my watch. It was 1300 hours. Only three more hours and we would have a lock on the tournament. The crew resumed some very purpose-ful chumming.

During those final three hours, there were four hook-ups, none of them on *Misty*. One fish was dropped within ten minutes, and two of the other three were taken. With each report, I noticed the *Misty* crew becoming more seriously involved with the task of "chopping and plopping," hoping for another hook-up.

At 1600 hours, the announcement from the committee boat: "The tournament is officially ended. There have been two fish taken so far today, with one still being fought. If there are any hook-ups after this announcement, they will be ineligible as a tournament fish. Good luck to all the boats at the final weigh-in."

I started the engine and sent the mate forward to haul the anchor. We seemed to be rocked-down, so Allen joined Ray on the bow to lend a hand. They cleated off the rode and, after a little persuasion by the use of the engine, we broke loose and the two of them proceeded to haul aboard not only our anchor, but another anchor as well. The other anchor had 20 feet of chain and about 100 feet of new 5/8 inch nylon.

Allen looked up from the bow and gave a thumbs-up sign. "We're on a roll, Cap. This ground tackle has to be worth four or five hundred bucks. So… let's go see if we have this tournament won!"

On the way back to the harbor, word came that the third fish had been tail-wrapped, giving us a three-to-one chance of winning.

As soon as we were tied up in our slip, we rushed over to the weigh-in to have a look at the competition. One of the fish on the ground would barely make 600 pounds, thereby making our odds two-to-one. The fish being hung on the scale looked as if it were a close contender, and we held our breath as the weigh-master called out, "Eight hundred and… let me make sure – yes, that's right – eight hundred and nine pounds."

My crew let out a collective combination of sound, somewhere between a cheer and a sigh of relief. Now it was down to a one-on-one battle between our fish and the last one that was just now arriving in the pick-up pit.

When the last fish was finally hung from the scale, it looked like a twin to ours – maybe a little longer, but not as fat. The weigh-master called out,

"Eight hundred and twenty one pounds." Allen, his son, my mate and I were crestfallen. Our hopes, after having led the tournament with the first fish on the first day until the last fish

Misty retur ns to Gr een Harbor and heads to the tour nament "pit."

on the last day, were yanked out from under us. The let-down, after three days of anticipation, was a very hard adjustment.

I swallowed hard, walked over to the other skipper to shake his hand and offer my congratulations. (afterwards, I thought of how much we must have looked, and felt, like something from a scene on TV, where the coaches of rival teams meet at mid-field to shake hands after a close contest).

The most remarkable thing about this tournament was the fact that there was only a twelve-pound difference separating the top three fish!

At the annual banquet that October, *Misty's* angler and crew received a small second-place trophy and plaque, the sizes of which did not reflect how close our entry had come to winning. The winner's trophy was over three feet tall.

There was one more trophy awarded that night… and it will always be my favorite. It was given to the skipper of the only boat ever to have fought and lost a "titanic battle with the fearsome Humpback whale of Stellwagen Bank." It was a six inch ceramic ash tray in the likeness of a whale, with an ingratiating grin and, if you look closely, you can see a tiny gold hook painted on its right pectoral fin.

Chapter 12

Manny Phillips, Master Fisherman

"fisherman n., ply. –men 1. a person who fishes for sport or a living."

This is the definition given in the New World Dictionary of the American Language. How totally inadequate this definition is when you think about what it takes to become a fisherman! Learning this intricate, ever-evolving craft can take an entire lifetime and, even then, many who pursue this discipline never even learn to cut bait.

Capt. Manny Phillips and I first exchanged greetings by radio, in August of 1970, the same year we both began our charter services. But, it wasn't until a blustery day in May of 1998 that I actually had a chance to sit down face-to-face with this notable gentleman.

Manny was the kind of man you like, instinctively, right away. He was stocky and solid, projecting strength, with an underlying hint of benevolence.

His face revealed the results of a lifetime of exposure to the sun and sea; yet his eyes, soft, somewhat secretive, and suggesting an inner curiosity, belied his age.

The Early Years

Manny was born in Provincetown, Mass., in 1918, the third of seven children. His father arrived in Nova Scotia from Portugal in 1914, by freighter. The vessel was denied entrance into Halifax Harbor because of its cargo of immigrants. Manny's father was literally given the choice of going back to Portugal, or floating ashore in a barrel on the incoming tide. He chose the latter.

He found a transportation "system," from Halifax to Boston that operated somewhat like the underground railroad such as that which helped Southern slaves find their way to freedom in the North, during the Civil War. From Boston, he made his way to Provincetown, mostly on foot.

After three years, with the help from the local Portuguese community and many days of hard work, fishing the Grand Banks, Manny's father was able to send for his family. His wife, son and daughter were all born in Portugal. Manny was the first of the growing family to be born in America.

For the next 13 years, Manny's father and oldest brother, John, fished the George's Bank aboard sailing schooners. As Manny grew, he increased his share of helping the family by learning the trade, and fishing when he wasn't in school. Since Manny was the first male family member born in America, his father was insistant that he complete his education. But, as it turned out, this was not to be.

Tragedies

The smaller fishing boats along Cape Cod began switching to gasoline power in the early decades of the 20th century. The first engines were typically "one lungers" with a heavy fly-wheel that kept the shaft turning until the cylinder reached its next power stroke.

In 1935, Manny's older brother, John, was killed. While he was working at the town pier gas dock, there was a gasoline explosion, probably caused by careless smoking during a refueling. The fire completely destroyed the Town Pier, a catastrophe that resulted in new laws to make boat engines safer. Yet, even today, we read about explosions at gas docks. (It seems some boaters are still careless.)

Three years later, tragedy struck the Phillips family again. Manny's younger brother, Clarence, and his father were seining for mackerel just south of No Man's Land (known to local fishermen simply as No Man's), a small island, south of the southwest corner of Martha's Vineyard.

It was September of 1938, and Massachusetts was about to receive a punishing blow by a huge hurricane that would roar through New England before retreating out to sea.

Manny's father never ventured very far from his homeport, unless he was accompanied by at least one other vessel from P'town. On this afternoon, the other vessel, while hauling back in mounting seas, fouled its rudder and propeller in its own net. With the loss of steerage, it soon broached and rolled over. In his attempt to rescue his friends, Manny's father's vessel took several big waves over the gunwales and foundered. His friend's vessel sank quickly, taking with it her captain and crew.

Now, unable to save his own boat, Manny's father and Clarence abandoned ship and were soon separated by the fury of the wind and sea. Clarence's body was never recovered, and he was listed as "drowned at sea". Manny's father swam northward toward The Vineyard, and eventually was found on the beach. He was unconscious, covered with cuts and bruises, with several broken bones. After his recovery on the island, he returned to P'town and continued to fish well into his seventies. Manny told me that he had "never known a tougher man" than his own father.

On His Own

Manny was just entering his junior year in high school when his father died and he had to assume the major responsibility for the support of his mother and four sisters. He quit school and started drift-net fishing for mackerel. A year later, he had his own boat and was fishing from Chatham, at the elbow of Cape Cod.

By 1944, he had moved up to a 56 foot dragger, which he named *Cape Cod* because, at that time, Manny said, "There was no reason to go any further than local waters." There was an abundance of marketable fish, all year around, within 20 miles of P'town. Fish were available to any fisherman willing to change his methods and gear with each new season. By this time, Manny had become THE P'town high-liner.

In 1950, Manny was approached by a gentleman from the Midwest, who wanted to use mackerel for feed on his mink farm (the oily mackerel produces fine, healthy and shiny fur). Manny accepted the farmer's offer and had a 70-foot dragger, built to his specifications, in St. Augustine, Florida. He named his new vessel, appropriately, the *Silver Mink.*

Mackerel were so plentiful during the '50s that Manny had no trouble filling the fish-hold after only two or three ten-minute trolls. This allowed plenty of time to use the Silver Mink to pursue cod and pollock, between filling orders for mink food.

Bluefin Tuna Times

Manny and the *Silver Mink* were hired, in 1952, by the federal Fish & Wildlife Administration to catch bluefin tuna for scientific research. About the same time, a cannery in Eastport, Maine

Manny's *Silver Mink*, the first tuna seiner, with schooner observing

said it would pay him ten cents a pound for all the tuna he could ship. These two offers, coming one right after the other, set off bells in Manny's head. The waters were teeming with tuna. Only a few boats were fishing them, and those were sport boats, only interested in catching one at a time. No one had tried to net these powerful fish – fish that were too fast and too smart to be caught by dragging. "Maybe," Manny speculated, "a purse net could be modified to handle these creatures."

Manny went to the West Coast, looking for purse nets, and while there, he met a fisherman named Yank Cazeroff. Yank had just such a net and was intrigued by the prospect of seining bluefin. They immediately liked and understood each other, so when Manny returned to P'town, he brought both the net and Yank.

After much modification, experimentation, and trial and error, they developed the know-how to make the purse work. Speaking of work: at the time, all hauling was done by hand, which accounts for Manny's Popeye-like forearms. (I always liked that term, "by hand," which when literally translated really means muscle-training, back-breaking labor.)

In 1955, Manny became the first boat-owner in P'town to use a power-winch. He bolted a winch to the deck with a chain, much like those used on bicycles, leading to a drum. With this ingenious rig, he was able to use the winch to close the purse seine and wind the net around the drum for storage until the next set.

Another first for this innovative fisherman was the use of an airplane to spot schools of tuna. Manny would often ride along with the spotter pilot to satisfy his constant curiosity about the lives of the bluefin. Manny became so intrigued by his personal observations that he obtained his private pilot's license and purchased his own plane. (He owned a Cessna 172, and a Piper Super Cub)

Spotting fish was the number one priority, but often, he went aloft just to observe tuna behavior, which helped him to better understand and appreciate their movements, and to "think like a fish." The year was 1957.

About this time, a friendly rivalry began with another leading P'town fisherman, Charley Mayo, father of "Stormy" Mayo, the now leading marine biologist for the Center for Coastal Studies, based in Provincetown. (see Chapter 21 for a story about Stormy's green tuna)

Both Manny and Charley were slightly stubborn, and both of them had strong views about how to fish for tuna. Those strong views eventually caused the start of a feud that lasted well into the 1980s. Charley was dead-set against purse seining, feeling it was an unfair way of taking tuna, while Manny had always had the conviction that any method was fair game, as long as it didn't deplete the resource. Both opinions had validity then and are still as true now as they were then, nearly 50 years ago. This controversy still splits the fishing community to this day. (My own feud about methods, with Capt Hebert, ended as soon as he handed me a live handline.)

Manny and Charley actually liked one another, and each respected the other's opinion. Still, every time the feud seemed to be coming to closure, they would find a new reason to take opposite sides again.

Manny was almost exclusively a tuna fisherman from 1955 through the 1960s, ever continuing to upgrade and perfect the methods he used to seine bluefin, while at the same time observing and learning the tuna's *modus operandi.*

For the most part, he was intrigued by his observations, although some years later, he would be appalled and sickened by a tuna killing frenzy that would take place in P'town Harbor.

Thoughts About Tuna

Manny realized the tuna were getting larger each year. This suggested that the same schools were returning to the same areas each year. He once told me that tuna are just as much creatures of habit as we humans.

This behavior pattern, called "imprinting" by marine biologists, can be observed and documented easily with long-lived marine mammals at the top of the food chain (whales, dolphins, seals, etc.) Biologists photograph and identify the same individuals on the same grounds, year after year. We could speculate, but were not sure if imprinting occurred in fish, other than salmon. (However, with the increased interest in tagging, we are now learning much more about the movements and habits of other species further down the food chain.)

Manny's observations about bluefin tuna have since proved to be correct, as the giants (600 lbs or more) have gradually been fished out. Each year, the average weight of bluefin caught in the western Atlantic declined, while at the same time, there appear to be more juvenile recruits mixed in the stock. These two observations suggested to Manny that a new, younger stock of tuna were being imprinted to return each year to the Northeast United States waters. (In 2002, huge numbers of "footballs" showed up in the gulf of Maine. They are returning each year a little bigger and stronger.)

Two Memorable Days

The 1960 season proved to be a bonanza for Manny, and he was sure that season would never be surpassed. When he tallied up the catch for that year, the *Silver Mink* has boated 1,100 metric tons of tuna. (The entire quota for all the tuna categories was lowered to 800mt in 1982 by ICCAT)

How wrong his prognostications proved to be! The next year, Manny's total tuna catch was about the same. And then, in 1962, an event took place that surprised Manny and the crew of the *Silver Mink* – an event so monumental that it would not be surpassed until the modern-day seiners, with their aircraft, electronics, high-powered net boats, and some 20 crew members, including expert divers, came into the fishery.

One morning as Manny was leaving the harbor, in the predawn light he could see the water ahead dancing with activity. From the P'town entrance buoy #3 to Corn Hill (a distance of almost four nautical miles), from the shore, westward, about a half-mile, the water was alive with feeding bluefin. After making the first set, he realized he would need lots of help. Manny radioed four other draggers, who had not yet gotten underway, to elicit their help. By mid-afternoon, he had filled all four of them to the gunwales.

At 9 p.m., after loading the *Silver Mink* for the last time that day with the remaining fish, he returned to the fish pier. That one 16-hour day had yielded 156 tons of tuna!

A second memorable catch occurred in '64 or '65, which was the complete reverse of the event of 1962. This time, the Silver

Mink wound up with only three or four fish, and Manny almost lost his boat.

One of the local draggers informed Manny that the SE corner of Stellwagen Bank had a big charge of fish, and it might be worth his while to check it out. By mid-morning, the next day, *Silver Mink* was deploying her net around an acre of fish, all of which were in the 500-pound range.

He was thinking it was a good thing the sea was flat-ass calm, because boating a big catch of this size fish would be impossible if the seas were running.

He and his crew had finished the set and almost had the seine cinched, when Manny noticed a large offshore dragger bearing down on them from the east. It was obvious that his boat was in for some real rockin' and rollin' from the wake being thrown by the oncoming trawler.

Being tightly secured to a net, cinching together tons of fish not effected by wave action, while a boat is tossed by a six to eight-foot wake would be akin to being cinched to the east side of a stone jetty during a Nor'easter.

Manny and crew quickly began cutting the seine free as the first wake reached the *Silver Mink*, lifting and rolling her into the net. Green water poured over the gunwale and then, just as quickly, she slipped into the trough and rolled to her other side, tearing free of most of the other lines that held her to the seine. Certainly, there was a mixture of cursing and praying from Manny and the crew as the dragger continued on its way. Prayers of thanks came as they realized they still had a deck underfoot!

As Manny finished telling the story, a curl began to show at the corners of his mouth, and the lines of his wrinkled face deepened. I noticed a twinkle appear in Manny's eyes as he began to chuckle, and I was puzzled. Here was a tale about almost losing his boat – and possibly his life and the lives of his crew along with losing several tons of dying tuna. (When fish are tightly packed, unable to move, with their gills held closed, they soon suffocate.) I asked how come he was smiling and chuckling.

Manny replied that when he returned to port and the story got around to the fleet, some of the enterprising dragger men left port and headed for Stellwagen Bank. The next three days was the only time that draggers have ever been successful at dragging for bluefin. (bluefin are one of very few species of fish that sink to the bottom when dead.)

Trolling

By 1970, Manny had designed a charter vessel which he had custom built to his specifications. The *Shady Lady*, along with Capt. Joe Eldridge's *Striper* soon became the pride of the burgeoning Cape Cod charter boat fleet.

In the early '70s, there were very few private sport fishing

Manny Phillips' *Shady Lady* charter boat

boats engaged in the tuna fishery, and with large numbers of striped bass available, no charter boats were targeting tuna. Tackle limitations were those endorsed by the International Game Fish Association (IGFA). The prevailing thoughts were that tuna was only for the "rich." This situation changed around 1975, when captains Manny and Joe began offering tuna charters to their customers.

They were still the only charter fishermen doing tuna charters, when two events occurred in 1976 that caused a profound change in the tuna fishery: The enactment of the Magnuson Fishery Conservation and Management Act (commonly called the 200-mile limit, but oh, so much more. .. See Chapter 2) The sudden increase in the value of the bluefin, brought about by the Japanese appetite for raw tuna, changed many fishermen's lives and attracted thousands of participants to what became "tuna mania".

Manny spent the early years of his charter service refining and perfecting his trolling technique. Near the end of the decade,

Captain Manny Phillips

Manny and Charley again found fuel for their ongoing feud. This time, it was over the proper way to catch tuna one-at-a-time. Manny stuck to trolling, while Charley insisted that handlining, with the enticement of chum, was the only ways to go. Actually, their feud was pretty much academic; after all, they were both high-liners within their chosen methods.

Throughout the '80s and '90s, I was offering "combo trips" – a half-day of chumming for tuna, followed by a half-day of fishing for blues. Manny, always the innovator was doing the same thing. Except, his combo was reversed. He would catch his blues first, and then troll with the smaller ones, either sewn into daisy chains or on a bar-rig, for bluefin.

Talk about innovation: During this period, Manny had his dog, a toy schnauzer, onboard most of the time. As *Misty* trolled by the *Shady Lady*, I could see his mate swinging an umbrella-rig full of blues over the transom and into the boat, while at the same time, Manny could be seen in his bridge enclosure with his beloved pet under one arm, while watering his tomato plants with the other. (The idea of growing tomatoes in the bridge enclosure makes perfect sense, after all. It makes an excellent green-house)

Earned His Titles

This gentleman's big heart finally came to rest in the New England Medical Center, on May 25, 2001, just two years after our only sit-down-face-to-face meeting.

Married for some 58 years to his wife, Germaine, with ten grandchildren and sixteen great-grand children, he answered to the name, "Pa Pa".

His always active and innovative mind had a profound impact on the tuna fishery from its inception, in 1952, when the Fish and Wildlife Administration hired him to catch tuna for scientific research. Manny had an amazing 50-years of influencing and shaping his chosen life's love – for instance:

• He developed the purse seine and the method for seining the mightiest of all fishes — by hand.

• He developed and used a winch – the first hauler – to cinch and haul the tuna net.

• Used aircraft to find and observe the habits of tuna.

• Became the leading skipper, using the trolling method, to hook and land tuna by rod and reel. (his success percentage was in the nineties).

• He even helped the mink industry to produce better and more beautiful pelts.

Captain Manny Phillips was an engaging and thoroughly charming personality, who I am proud to have known throughout the last three decades of the 20 th century. He is one of the very few men that I have know in my lifetime who really earned the title of "Fisherman." Here's to you, Captain Manny Phillips — as far as I'm concerned, you will always be the "PaPa".

Chapter 13

Joe Eldridge, The Master Rod & Reeler

This story is written about and dedicated to the memory of Captain Joe Eldridge of Barnstable, Massachusetts. He was a soft-spoken, kindly gentleman, who always gave more to life than he asked of it. He was as well know within the fishing community as his nephew, Todd Eldridge is know throughout the ice-skating community. Todd is a world-class champion, and his uncle Joe was a world-class master of his chosen field. Capt. Joe was a Cape-Codder and a man of the sea, and above all, a superb FISHERMAN.

I first became acquainted with Capt. Joe Eldridge in the mid-sixties when I called him on the CB radio, asking for some help in locating a school of striped bass. I'd heard a charge of big stripers had shown up on Billingsgate Shoals, northeast of Sesuit Harbor on the north side of Cape Cod. I was fishing near the entrance buoy, two miles north of the Harbor, and having no luck at all. It was still early. The sun had not yet burned off the thick morning fog. Capt. Joe came back to me right away and, in his soft-spoken manner, asked my location. Then, he simply said, "come due north about two miles. The fish are in thirty feet of water."

The result of this short and concise reply produced a memorable morning of fishing that included several fish in the 30-pound range. Over the next two decades, I experienced many other occasions that heightened my respect and admiration of this man's expertise.

About once in a lifetime, if we are lucky, we become acquainted with a man on the fishing scene who brings a whole new meaning to the word "fisherman," a man who is the very essence and embodiment of the true meaning of the word. He understands and appreciates all the creatures of the sea, and through years of experience, hones his fishing skills to a point where he seems to have a sixth sense about those creatures. When he hooks-up, he immediately knows the who-what-where-when-and-why of the creature on the terminal end. In short, such men learn to "think like a fish".

Capt. Joe gained an early reputation as a charter skipper specializing in striper fishing. He was known up and down the east coast as "Striper Joe." All of his boats were built to his own specifications, and of course, were all named *Striper*.

By the early '70s, he was also considered the best rod and reel tuna fisherman on the Atlantic coast. I remember watching with amazement as he once unwrapped a bluefin from around four anchor lines, and walked him out of the fleet as if there was nothing in his way!

That day, *Striper* was anchored on the SW corner of Stellwagen Bank, north of *Misty*. There was one boat anchored between us. All the boats along the steep edge of the Corner were facing into a mild breeze from the west.

I was on the bridge, taking a break, while the mate was handling the chumming chores. Ray glanced up at the bridge and pointed toward *Striper*. "Striper Joe seems to be hooked up." Joe had dropped his anchor ball, snubbed the fish as though it were a dog on a very short leash. He was backing down hard to take the fish aft of the boat anchored between us. I don't think the crew of that boat knew *Striper* was hooked-up until he had walked the fish more than halfway down their starboard side, maneuvering Striper well past their transom to clear their deployed hand lines.

Joe suddenly kicked *Striper* into gear, spun her around and headed straight toward my boat. I leaped from the bridge and was standing on the foredeck with my quick-release in hand; ready to let go, as *Striper* approached my starboard quarter. As Joe passed from stern to bow along my starboard side, I asked him to let me know when to let go my anchor line. He put *Striper* hard over to port, spun around my bow, and continued down my port side, as he calmly said, "No need, Cappy. We have him right where we want him."

He repeated the procedure with the boat to my south'ard. Then, after taking the fish around the stern of the next boat, he steered it between the next two boats and calmly walked it out of the fleet and into the deep water to the west.

This incident taught me how to use my vessel as a way to direct and control the activities of a hooked tuna – and that a boat can often be your most valuable fishing tool.

Joe knew where that fish was at all times and, by anticipating its next move, was able to keep it under control throughout the march from hook-up to clearing the fleet. The ensuing struggle lasted only 40 minutes more, before Joe had the fish tail-roped.

Most tuna men have no idea what their hooked fish is doing early on in the fight; some even have no clue even when the fight reaches the latter stages. Capt. Joe's ability to "read" the fish from the git-go was a rare gift, indeed.

Joe was as giving a fisherman as I've ever known. He willingly shared his knowledge with any and all other fishermen. When he knew he was right, he was very emphatic; leaving no doubt in anyone's mind that his knowledge and experience had come to the fore and his statement was the complete truth.

I had lost a fish after a seven-hour battle, and I told Capt. Joe about it. (Most of the struggle was brought about by the angler being unwilling to take suggestions from the mate and a refusal to share the angling with any other crewmember.) Joe fixed me with his look of disdain and said very softly, "Anytime you spend more than two hours on a fish, you are going to lose him, Cappy." With Joe, you learned to accept his words as fact and never questioned. This incident, which I stored in my mind for future reference, was just another piece of wisdom from the master.

Capt. Joe was always low-key, not only in his voice and actions, and he always went about this business of fishing in a very quiet and deliberate way. My fondest memory of him occurred on 18 August, on the first day of the Green Harbor Tuna Club Tournament of 1973.

I had booked a Mr. Allen Freer, his son Allen Jr., and a friend, Bob Coleby for the three-day tournament. At the captains' meeting on the night before the tournament was to begin, Allen and I made special note of some of the rules to be followed.

- Each day, as soon as practical, all tournament boats must report to the committee boat that they are fishing.
- All hook-ups must be reported to the committee boat as soon as circumstances allow.
- The tournament chairman must be informed when a fish is either tail-roped or lost.
- No lines in the water prior to 0800.
- No chum to be cast overboard prior to 0800.
- No chum to be flushed down the head prior to 0800.
- After 0800 chum as you wish.

The rest of the rules had to do with the 1973 IGFA rules and regulations pertaining to double lines, leaders, gaffs, etc.

By 0730 the next morning, we were anchored on the fishing grounds, preparing hooks, bait and chum for the 0800 start.

As soon as the announcement, "To all boats entered in the Green Harbor tuna tournament, you may commence fishing." came over the VHF, all baits were deployed and some very heavy chumming began.

I reported *Misty* in as fishing and then assigned each crewmember their duties for the hook-up. It was 0820 when I climbed to the bridge and began going over my mental check-list, to make sure I had covered all the bases. I had only reached second base when Allen yelled, "We're on" as he picked up the rod and set the hook. The crew cleared the other lines and very shortly we walked the fish out of the fleet.

I reported the hook-up to the committee boat and a minute later heard Capt. Joe's familiar voice, "Go get him, Cappy! Do you mind if I jump on your anchor ball?"

"You're welcome, anytime, Joe. Go right ahead" was my reply. I noticed *Striper* coming toward the fleet from the direction of the Cape Cod Canal. Nothing more needed to be said. Capt. Joe wanted to get his day's fishing started, and I was going to be very busy with the fish.

Allen was short and stocky, with the powerful arms of a man who spent much of his life working in heavy construction. I didn't have to worry about this angler pooping out on me halfway through the fight.

For the first hour, the fish was very active, remaining near the surface and doing a "first I'll give a little, then I'll take a little" routine. Allen was right there with the fish, getting as much line as the fish would allow, and then keeping the rod tip high to maximize the pressure when it was stripping line from the reel.

I had reported the hook-up at 0820 and it was now about 0940. We were well into our second hour when the fish changed his game plan. It went straight down for the bottom. I backed down hard toward the fish, in an attempt to counter its new tactic. Allen was able to gain line quickly and soon had the spool close to full. The line was almost straight up and down, directly off the stern, when our quarry "set his feet" and began making tight circles under the boat. Allen looked over his shoulder, said he had gained all of the line the fish was willing to give up, and asked me what to do next.

The radio barked, "To all boats fishing the Green Harbor Tuna Club tournament... the 10 o'clock report is as follows: There has been one hook-up, by *Misty*, with Allen Freer the angler. The chairman would like a status report from *Misty*."

This interruption annoyed me and I remember thinking how lucky for Joe that he didn't have to worry about radio reports, since he was not fishing the tournament. At this point, I felt like a golfer on the 18th green, looking at a 3-foot putt that will win the tournament, ready to stroke the ball when someone in the gallery sneezes. (When you are into a fish, you need all your concentration on the task at hand.)

I called the committee boat and reported, "The fish is straight down, and we estimate it to be 200 or 250 feet to the double line. Over." "Thank you, *Misty*. Good luck with the rest of the fight. Out."

I put the rudder amidships, pushed the shift forward, and told the crew I was going to try to plane the fish up, aft of the transom, to give Allen a chance to gain line when the fish nears the surface again. After a few minutes, the line was on a 45° angle. Allen began gaining line with slow and steady turns on the handle.

Ten minutes of this slow retrieval, and the double line came into sight. The mate had just taken his position between the footrest and the stern, ready to grab the double line and wire the fish to the starboard quarter, when the line suddenly went slack. With the sudden release of tension, the rod came up and gave Allen an embarrassing blow on his protruding jaw.

Allen cranked the double line onto the reel, all the way to the snap swivel. We could see the hook riding the first wake in the wash. I picked up the mike and called the committee boat. "We lost him. We just got the hook back with the double line in hand. Out."

Most boats rarely use the "Over" or "Out" terminology when using the VHF radio, but in this case, I wanted to let the fleet know I didn't wish to communicate any further.

I looked at my watch. 1015. The fish had been on for one hour and fifty-five minutes. A few minutes later, as we were approaching the fleet, I remembered Capt. Joe's admonition about spending no more than two hours on a fish. I called Joe. "Joe, we dropped him at about the two hour mark. I'm going to need my ball back." "I heard, Cappy. Too bad. I'll keep the slick going for you till you get near me."

This was typical of Captain Joe Eldridge. He would always go out of his way to help someone else get a fish, even if it meant he had to leave a choice area.

When we were 100 feet off the port side of *Striper*, Joe dropped my pick-up line and backed away, while his mate continued to chum heavily.

Capt. Joe's voice again on the VHF. "Cappy, thank you for the use of your ball. Better luck with the next one." As Capt. Joe said this, he turned hard to port and as *Striper* swung around, I was able to see his starboard side for the first time. My surprise turned immediately to admiration for this modest master. Hooked to his block and tackle, ready to be hoisted into the cockpit, was a bluefin tuna - 900 pounds minimum.

I'll always remember Capt. Joe Eldridge as a mild-mannered master of Rod & Reel tuna fishing, the perennial high-liner of striped bass fishing, a most knowledgeable and experienced fisherman, and an unparalleled teacher.

(Allen's 15-year old son angled an 812-pound fish later this same morning and you read the outcome of this tuna tournament in Chapter 11.)

The tuna seems to be preparing to tow Misty — everyone pays attention.

Chapter 14

Donald Hebert - Handline Authority

Captain Donald Hebert was born in Marshfield, Mass. in 1936. He attended Marshfield High School until age 16 when he married his high school sweetheart, Estelle, and dropped out of school to care for his new family. He settled into a home in Brant Rock, a section of Marshfield that borders on Cape Cod Bay, and what a family it became! By 1962, at the age of 26, Don was the father of six children, all boys: Donald Jr., Bruce, Danny, Kenny, Gary and Paul.

All the boys were brought up to work on and have respect for the sea. They all served as mates aboard Capt. Don's party boat *White Lady* as they matured (All but Donald Jr. also became mates aboard my charter boat *Misty*.)

Today, all but Danny are still involved with and making their living from the waters in and around Cape Cod Bay.

I was immediately fascinated by this man. Capt. Don was about 5' 8" tall, with a big barreled chest, slightly bow legged, with kind eyes that resonated a quiet intelligence. His voice had a soft hoarseness that made one think of the sound of a far off fog horn.

His forearms were as big around as an average man's thighs, and he had a standing challenge for any one to try to beat him at arm wrestling. I have watched Don in Haddad's bar and grille in Brant Rock, take on men who were a foot taller and out-weighed him by 100 pounds. He was never defeated and in most of these showdowns Don never even broke a sweat.

He would often bark but he kept his bite under control as if he knew his raw power could easily harm an opponent. When agitated or provoked, you could see Don coming to a boil and building a head of steam; he would verbally vent some of the pressure and then more than likely turn away and stroll off muttering to himself.

The first time I met this man, my impression was one of standoffish gruffness with a slight swagger of assurance. Don knew who he was and what he was about. Here was a man capable of thinking like a fish and from a very early age he knew he was going to spend his life pursuing every specie of finny creature indigenes to the North Atlantic coast.

Life's Work Begins

Capt. Don started his party boat fishing service in 1969 with a brand new boat built by Jessie Boats, Inc. of Plymouth, Massachusetts. He christened her *White Lady* and from the day of her launching she was to become his passion, his obsession and both his mistress and his master. Capt. Don had a love affair with *White Lady* that lasted into the '90s.

The following year I started my "six-pack" charter fishing service in the Green Harbor section of Marshfield, Mass., and for the next several seasons *White Lady* and *Misty* were the only boats from that port offering fishing excursions.

Captain Hebert's *White Lady* , with pulpit extension in place.

Now after 35 years of charter fishing, I have yet to see any head or charter boat, including my own, that obviously has received the tender-loving-care Capt. Don gave to *White Lady* year in and year out.

He had an uncanny knack for knowing where the fish were going to be and when they would be ready to start feeding. I've watched Don move *White Lady* into an area where several skippers were beginning to vacate because the bite was just not happening. One of the skippers would call Don and tell him there were no fish around; Don would proceed to anchor and then tell the caller that he was going to give it a try anyway. As the other boat moved away Don would tell his passengers to drop their rigs to the bottom and within minutes there would be bent rods on the White Lady and shouts to the mates to come and gaff their catch.

Working Together

Capt. Don and I began working together for our mutual benefit. If one of us was having a hard time finding fish, all that was necessary was to use the CB radio and we would receive a quick and honest response as to how the catch was and where the other boat was located. (I freely admit that I received much more help from our agreement than I was able to return to Capt. Don.)

In the early '70s we never worried about using the radio to help each other out; the huge numbers of fishermen we see today had not yet begun to proliferate and most of those who were fishing, it seems, hadn't yet discovered the CB radio as an important piece of fishing "gear."

In today's world with all the sophisticated electronics, (VHF radios, color SOUNDER, DGPS, RADAR and PLOTER) Capt. Don and I agree that using a radio will only reveal your exact position, but to a sharp skipper, also the course and distance to that location! Basically, there is only one way to try to protect that "honey hole"- - - - - - - stay off the VHF and use a cell phone or, when ashore, try the good old landline.

A Great Day

In the mid '70s Don and I had the good fortune to share one of those amazing fishing experiences that most fishermen only dream about. *White Lady* got underway at 0615 with a full compliment of passengers while *Misty* had to wait for the passenger who had booked my charter. He had gotten stuck in traffic behind an accident on the way to Green Harbor and was over half an hour late.

When *Misty* finely cleared the east jetty, I came around to the course for the "H" buoy and called Don to see if he had found the fish so I could make up the lost time. He answered with a short agitated sentence, "Not yet damn it." I continued my course toward the "H" some six NM ahead.

I was looking for fish along the 20-fathom curve south of the buoy when the CB barked again. "*Misty*, if you're not doing any fish you might want to come to Pollock Shoals." Short and succinct. I didn't have to reply; instead I hit the throttle and swung the bow to the west'ard.

As I approached Pollock Shoals, I could see myriads of birds. There were terns, gannets, shearwaters, storm petrels and black-back, herring, and laughing gulls. They were all franticly feeding at the "Pollock Shoals Diner." Their combined calls created a loud cacophonous noise as if each one of them was fighting for its share of the bounty. The surface beneath this frenzy was alive with sand eels and baitfish franticly trying to escape marauding fish from below.

White Lady was anchored in the middle of the one mile in diameter shoal and it looked as if all of the passengers had bent rods. I started a drift that would take *Misty* down the port side of *White Lady* and told my charter to drop their rigs. Before any of them reached the bottom all six rigs were tight to fish!

Two things happened by the end of our first hour on the shoal. First my anglers filled *Misty's* large insulated fish box with 500 lbs. of cod, haddock and pollock and then they decided to take a break from the "lift and crank" mode to give their arms a rest.

The mate began filleting the fish while the crew and I became observers of the vast variety of life that had come to feed at this huge lunch counter.

I saw several bluefin tuna cruising back and forth along the perimeter of the shoal to the east'ard and was about to call Don when I noticed he was already hauling anchor and making preparations to give chase. Nothing on the water ever occurred unnoticed by this fisherman.

The finale to this eventful day was when this seemingly limitless variety of life was joined by several pilot whales circling in the deep water just beyond the drop offs of Pollock Shoals. Pilot whales, (Most fishermen call them black fish.) are known to feed on sand eels whenever they are present and this day had them in prodigious amounts.

Hand Line Authority

By 1976 the Japanese market for bluefin tuna had made the fish very valuable. A fish that dressed out at 600 lbs. would bring the fisherman from 600 to 750 dollars. (The price of $1.25 per pound was very enticing in the mid 70s.) Capt. Hebert thought there had to be a more productive way to catch these precious creatures. After some thought and a little experimenting Don developed what was to become the "Tuna Hand Line." (Chapter 17 - Hand Line)

He was the fisherman who would return to Green Harbor with a fish almost every time he went tuna fishing. By the end of the 1976 tuna season Don was the high-liner, not only of his own port, but also of the entire tuna fleet. Don and the *White Lady* had proved that with the use of a hand line, by an accomplished fisherman, the success ratio of capturing fish could become seven out of ten hook-ups!

As noted in Chapter 17, Don and I had many arguments over the hand lines obvious ability to capture tuna. His statement that always ended the arguments — "Don't knock it till you've tried it." — was classic Capt. Hebert rhetoric, which usually had a double entendre! That one trip when Don handed me a hand line with a bluefin on the other end not only ended all of my arguments but also changed my tuna fishing preference. The following season I was offering tuna charters with hand lining as the preferred method.

Don's Delight

The 1978 tuna season began on time about the first week of June and I noticed that Don was always going to the grounds with a 16' lap strake surfboat in tow. The boat had a 10-horsepower outboard and had been used by Don as his tender.

Talk around the harbor was that Don was developing something new to improve his tuna take. Don was always innovative about his life's passion and I had learned that he was tight-

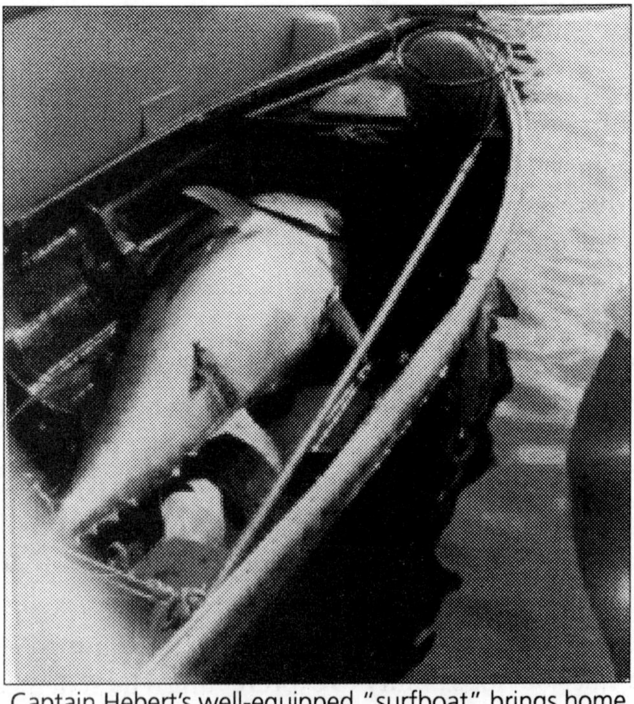

Captain Hebert's well-equipped "surfboat" brings home a good-sized bluefin.

lipped when working on a new idea.

One day in mid June I was anchored next to *White Lady* near the notch on the SW corner of Stellwagen Bank; my crew was intent on their chumming chores while I was intent on observing what was going on with Don and White Lady. His tender had been tied to the midship cleat on the port side so it would not interfere with the chum slick.

There was an audible "snap" and line pealed from one of *White Lady's* hand line baskets. Don grabbed the line and told Kenny (son #4) to bring the tender to the stern. Nobody went to the quick release to drop the anchor ball and nobody started the engine! I glanced at my watch - 0705. As soon as Kenny got the tender to the stern he put the basket and tuna ball in the tender and then took the hand line from Don, held the fish, while Don clambered into the tender. The Capt. grabbed the hand line, set the hook again and off he and tender sped. Here it was near the end of the Twentieth century and I was watching a one man "Nantucket Sleigh Ride."

Don very quickly pulled the boat to the fish and began to winch it to the surface. When the fish broke water, Don held it there with his left hand and reached for his cockpit harpoon with his right. The fish was held snug to the gunwale and his struggling could only scribe tight circles with the tender. One thrust with the harpoon and Don had his fish completely under control. It was now - 0727: just 22 minutes since Kenny brought the tender to the transom. The captain put a tail rope on his prize, started the engine, raked the gills to bleed the fish and sat on the center thwart with a satisfied grin as he made a short trip circling some of the boats from Green Harbor. Fishermen, who are also thinking innovators, deserve a chance to show off there inventive insight.

THE Pulpit

I always kidded Don's pronunciation of "pulpit" because he always said polepit. Come to think of it, he may be right, after all, he always used a "pole" when he was sticking fish from his pulpit. The pulpit on *White Lady* was eighteen feet long; just half of her over all length and the height of the stand stood ten above the water. Don was most comfortable using a stick of sixteen feet.

He loved harpooning tuna because the resultant fight was a one-on-one battle and he had the upper body strength to immediately let his opponent know who was in charge! His development of the hand line basket must have been a direct result of his experience with the harpoon.

Don Gets A Nose Job

Misty had a bluefish charter and we were trolling around the tuna fleet on the SW corner of Stellwagen Bank when I noticed *White Lady* approaching: she was obviously tracking a pod of tuna. Don was standing on the foredeck just in front of the windshield waiting for the proper time to head for the stand. He was on a course that would take him across *Misty's* stern.

I had a view of the pod just as Don went to the stand and aimed his stick almost straight down. One strong thrust and the harpoon came to an abrupt stop, bounced back up and the top caught Don square in the nose! He grasped the stick, threw again, and immediately buried it deep into his adversary. Line rushed from the basket as Don hurried down the pulpit with blood streaming from his nose and staining his white tee. The Capt. chased down the tuna ball and with no lost motion, winched the fish to the side of the boat, cinched a tail rope to him, hoisted the fish half way out of the water with his hauler and then proceeded to bleed the victim.

I waited about a half hour and called *White Lady*. "What happened, Don?" His reply: "My first shot missed, it bounced off his gill plate. I must have stunned him because he was still there. The son-of-bitch broke my nose so I buttonholed him with the second shot." This succinct answer sounded as if he had suddenly come down with a stuffy head cold. I found out why when *White Lady* passed us on its way to Green Harbor. Don waved to us with long paper towel streamers hanging like walrus tusks from his very swollen nose!

Hebert's Handy Ideas

Not content with his stand 18 feet ahead of *White Lady's* bow, Don added an additional 10-foot section ahead of the original stand and set the angle so his feet were now 15 feet above the surface when he was standing twenty-eight feet ahead of his boat's bow. He soon found out that this new set up increased his shot percentage and also consequently his tuna take.

The additional pulpit was pinned to the tip of the 18-footer so it could fold over the top, and then both could be lifted and secured to the superstructure when not in use.

Always trying to tweak his fishing performance, Don noticed that there were times when the fish would be actively feeding on his chum, coming up the slick eating every chunk except the pieces armed with the hooks. (Watching the fish approach in this mode is a maddening experience, especially when you make eye contact as they turn away at the transom with a slight smirk on their countenance. If tuna had hands instead of fins I'd be sure they were flipping me the finger!)

Capt. Don came up with his solution. He merely rigged his ten-foot pulpit extension to face aft from his cockpit- overhead. When on the stand, above and aft of his transom, he could watch a fish approach and harpoon it before the fish became aware of his presence!

Don had a state of the art sounder on *White Lady* but he always wondered what was in the water surrounding his boat; not just the water between its keel and the bottom. He came up with the answer to his inquisitiveness long before the advent of side-scan-sonar. He bought an extra transducer and an extension cable compatible with his sounder. He then taped the transducer to the end of a scrub brush handle and plugged the cable into the sounder. With this "Hebert-gadget," Don could place the transducer in the water and by rotating the brush end, he was able to scan the water all around the *White Lady.*

I watched Don using this "gadget" to pull a fish from the slick of the boat anchored next to him. He had the scrub brush control aimed at the other boat's transom and then began throwing chum chunks aft of its stern. Each toss was a little closer to one of *White Lady's* balloon floats and when the chum was beginning to reach it, the float disappeared and Don set the hook.

As soon as Don had the fish free of the fleet I called him and asked if he would mind if I jumped on his anchor ball? Don said, "Be my guest."

When *Misty* had settled on his ball, I began imitating Don's technique, trying to suck a fish from the other boat's slick. I saw a little flash of tuna belly just before the snap of one of my breaker strings and I was hooked-up. During the fight I kept thinking the skipper of the other boat must have been wondering how he became the victim of de-je-vue all over again.

Tuna have excellent vision and a great sense of smell. However their auditory acumen and sense of feeling seem to work together. This last fact didn't get by the Capt's inquisitive mind. What could be done in this area to attract tuna? One thing that is a true attractant to all fish species is when bait fish splash on the surface making a sound akin to a sudden rainsquall over water. How do you duplicate a rainsquall sound on a bright sunlit day - on demand?

Don's answer? Rig the salt-water wash-down hose to the tip of your outrigger, deploy the outrigger, and merely turn on the water pressure. With the nozzle adjusted for a medium spray, both the look and the sound are surprisingly close to the real thing. The Captain found out that using this fake "baitfish splashing" enabled him to pull even more fish from other boat's chum slicks. I told him that if he kept developing his gadgets he would start catching tuna without the use of bait or chum. Don answered by reminding me that he had been doing just that ever since he harpooned his first fish from his "polepit."

Captain Donald Hebert has been a friend and mentor of mine ever since the mid 70s. This chapter only reflects a small portion of the innovative ideas and developments he brought to the fishing community over the last three decades. Don also had an ambiguous trait, in that he would share almost any of his ideas with his fishing buddy's while at the same time being very secretive with anybody he felt had not "paid their dues" by putting in their time. (This of course included all those who would never have a clue, even after double-timing their time on the blue.)

Today Don can reflect on his amazing career while the dues he has paid with the years of fishing a full season of nine months, (Consisting of sport and bottom chartering, dragging for cod and pollock, commercial striped bass & blue fishing, and of course his expertise with the king - bluefin tuna.) finds himself with full blown arthritis.

He never did anything having to do with the love of his life — *White Lady* — in a half-ass manner.

There are many fishermen of today who owe this man a big THANKS because they are doing things and using gear that Don designed or developed. They have no idea that Captain Donald Hebert is the one "who-dun-it" originally. Over the years I have learned more about fishing from him than any other member of the fishing community.

This chapter is to celebrate Don's experimental and innovative career. One of the luckiest things in my life is the friendship I have had with this captivating captain, companion, and curmudgeon.

Chapter 15

The Hat Trick & The Chum Ladle

The skipper was always pleasant, cheerful and outgoing; the kind of friend who would give you the shirt off his back. He was knowledgeable about boats and he kept his 30-footer, *The Rogue*, in immaculate condition. He had a deep respect for the sea, and above all, was a good fisherman. Everybody liked this man.

"Faults?" you ask. Only one, and that wasn't a detriment. The skipper talked too much. He could turn a simple question with a simple answer into a half hour discussion of last year's season. His modus operandi was always, "if one word will suffice, use ten." In fact, he became known as "Captain Motor Mouth" or "Capt. Mouth" for short. Only once was he ever stopped short, and unable or unwilling to continue a conversation. It happened during a fishing trip, very late in August, neat the SW corner of Stellwagen Bank, in Cape Cod Bay.

Capt. Mouth was a rod and reel fisherman, who preferred trolling fresh bait. He looked down on all tuna-men who would lower themselves to the use of that "rotten, foul-smelling chum".

The first weeks of August had been very hot and dry. The bulk of the fish had settled in at the SW corner, and were feeding heavily on chum. There had been no reports of any fish being taken by any other method for almost three weeks; and a month had passed since Capt. Mouth had even had a hook-up.

The skipper had a crew of two; his best friend, Bud, and an experienced mate. They had been with him for three seasons and they had their act together as far as trolling was concerned. Both crew members had long since learned to survive a day aboard *The Rogue* by listening abstractly to the constant barrage of verbiage, and making sure they never added anything to the conversation

As the fishless days went by, the balance of discussion began to even out. The crew became bolder about urging the captain to try chumming. At the end of another week of frustration, while they were tying the boat in its slip, Capt. Mouth announced nonchalantly that they would be "chumming" tomorrow. An hour later, after cleaning the boat, storing the chum in a cooler, and preparing the "soup" (a mixture of ground up herring, cod liver oil and sea water) in a five gallon bucket, he was still explaining just how and why he had come to this conclusion.

The next morning, when Bud arrived, there was a note from the mate propped against the compass. "Forgot to tell you, it's my sister's wedding day. Can't make it. Good luck chumming." Bud thought to himself, "short, concise, and to the point. I wonder what the skipper will make of it?"

Capt. Mouth arrived right on time and, as usual, muttering to himself. He read the note, looked at Bud and said only, "Damn."

As Bud waited for the dissertation to begin, the captain removed a sterling silver soup ladle from a tote bag and placed it on the tackle locker. Bud knew it would be best not to inquire, but he had to ask anyway, "What the hell is that for?"

"It's my wife's favorite soup ladle. I'm not going to touch that chum. I thought that since we'd made "chum soup" it might be appropriate to bring this along. It will make the task easier. Besides... if we ———." He was still pontificating about the use of the ladle as *The Rogue* cleared the end of the jetty and he pushed the throttle to cruising speed.

The roar of the engine brought a measure of relief to Bud, as he set about opening the flats of chum so they could begin to thaw.

After arriving at the Bank, while the boat was settling on its anchor, it was agreed that the chumming duties would alternate between the captain and Bud, each hour. The hook baits were deployed and Capt. Mouth began his hour of "chop and plop", while muttering something about the mate going to a wedding on this very day, when he could be here, doing this nasty work.

About every ten or twelve chunks of herring, the skipper would put down the knife, stir the "soup" with the silver ladle, and then broadcast two full scoops overboard, one each, to port and starboard. All the while, he muttered about how this was sure to draw fish into their slick.

When Bud took over the "chop and plop" duties, he began doubling the use of the ladle - two scoops to port and two scoops to starboard – not just to change the captain's routine, but to get rid of the "soup" that much quicker. (If at all possible, don't ever get downwind of day-old "chum soup.") Bud was sure the silver ladle was already starting to tarnish!

Twenty minutes later, one of the balloons went under and the line screamed off the reel of the rod set in the port quarter rod-holder.

After clearing the other lines, Bud started the engines, dropped the anchor ball, and climbed to the bridge, ready to use his considerable experience at *The Rogue*'s helm, to once again handle the boat from hook-up to successful capture.

Capt. Mouth had taken the strike and settled into the fighting chair; yelling about things that should be done, "Don't forget to start the engines before you pull the quick-release to the anchor ball. Did you clear the lines on the starboard quarter? Who's going to steer the chair with you at the helm and the mate not here?" Etc, etc.

Bud calmly walked the fish out of the fleet, between two boats, and allowed it to take them a mile to the west. Far enough to insure them solitude for the upcoming fight.

Capt. Mouth immediately began again with his usual oral diarrhea, "This seems like a big fish. Let's make him tow the boat. Get me my gloves. Come down and put the cover on the 'soup,' it's getting ripe. Don't bother rinsing off the ladle." And, so on and so on and so on.

It was soon apparent that this fish was not going to be taken easily. Bud acted on the captain's advice, only when it pertained to using the boat effectively. He continued to make the right moves as needed, but ignored all of the other suggestions that really had nothing to do with gaining the upper hand over the bluefin.

At the end of an hour, several things had taken place: The fish had gained his second wind and was towing the boat, seemingly effortlessly. Capt. Mouth was still making with the uninterrupted verbiage. Bud realized the skipper was beginning to tire, and noticed that the harangue was being directed more toward him than the fish. Capt. Mouth was now asking Bud to come down and take over the angling duties. Over the next several minutes, the asking changed to a demand, then to a command.

Bud was a very patient man, easy going and slow to anger; but even the most patient men have limits. As the tirade continued, Bud suddenly, and uncharacteristically, shouted from the bridge, "Shut up and catch that fish! I'm tired of your yelling and I'm not going to relieve you!"

This outburst didn't slow the skipper's tempo, but it did change his strategy from demanding, to begging. "Please Bud, I can't gain any line. I'm exhausted. We'll lose the fish if you don't come down and relieve me. My arms are tired. Please, please, pleeeeeeeze!"

As the talking continued, unabated, Bud became more and more agitated; not so much because the captain was still running off at the mouth, but because he seemed to have given up on the fish. Bud considered this and decided he was not going to take over the angler's duties, even if it did mean loosing the fish, and possibley a good friend.

"At least come down and give me a drink. I'm hot, and sweaty. Maybe you could pour some water over my head also? Please, please. Pleeeeeze give me some relief!"

Bud had reached the end of his rope. He quickly descended from the bridge, looked at the skipper's sweaty face, and then removed the captain's hat. "You want cool? Here's cool!" And with that, he proceeded to dump a ladle-full of chum soup on the captain's head. Then, after replacing the captain's hat, he pulled it tightly down and beat a hasty retreat to the safety of the bridge!

At first, there was silence. Next came a stream of invectives that Bud had never heard the captain use before, interlaced with some words that Bud was sure the skipper had never uttered before. All the while, Capt. Mouth was somehow able to hold the rod with one hand, while using his free hand to wipe the vile soup from his eyes, and dig the lumps from his ears.

When he finally stopped to take a breath, his silence was followed by renewed physical activity. As he began to pump the rod and gain line, he muttered, almost to himself, "When I get this fish, I'm going to beat the shit out of you with it." Next came the orders – how to handle the boat during the fight.

Bud shut out the harangue emanating from the cockpit, and put all his concentration into maneuvering *The Rogue* to counter the actions of the fish. Another fifteen minutes and the combination of Bud's expertise and the renewed, hostile and angry energy of the skipper brought the spent bluefin to within thirty feet of the transom.

When Bud was sure the fish was ready to be taken, he dropped the engine into idle, quickly descended from the bridge, harpooned and tail-roped it – all without saying a word – and then retreated again to the safety of the bridge.

The ride back to the harbor was notable for two reasons: First, Capt. Mouth never asked for the helm, preferring to stay in the cockpit; secondly, and more importantly, for the lack of conversation.

The skipper never once looked up at the bridge, and never said a word to Bud for the entire hour and a half it took to return to Green Harbor.

Bud could hear some low mutterings now and then from below, but it was in a very subdued volume and indiscernible. It was as if the skipper had suddenly come down with a bad case of vocal constipation.

At the helm, Bud began to speculate as to his fate. Had he

blown their long-lasting friendship, with that silver ladle full of chum? Would there be a nasty confrontation back at the pier? Was this to be their last fishing trip together? Was the Mouth really going to kick the shit out of him when they reached port?

After the fish was offloaded and weighed, Bud pulled into the slip and Capt. Mouth secured *The Rogue* to its finger pier. Bud noted that the skipper was completely silent, not even mumbling to himself. This could be good news, or bad. Bud went about his usual duties, glancing every now and then at Capt. Mouth, wondering when the explosion of rage would occur.

Bud turned-to, performing all the little tasks that a good mate learns to do each time a boat returns to port; check the fuel level, test the automatic bilge pump floats, look over the engines for any leaks, check the oil levels in the engines and transmissions, and check both water and oil filters. All the while, he was listening for any change in Capt. Mouth's quiet demeanor.

The utter silence continued as they worked together, scrubbing the gurry odor from *The Rogue,* washed down the rods and reels, and stowed all the gear.

Bud was not about to ask the skipper what his plans were for the next day's fishing, preferring not to stir up the rage he was sure Capt. Mouth was struggling to keep in check.

When Bud swung his leg over the gunwale to depart, Capt. Mouth suddenly broke his silence. Smiling broadly, he grabbed Bud's hand and declared, "Good job with the boat. See you tomorrow at 0530 sharp."

As he headed up the ramp toward his Jeep, Bud scratched his head in disbelief at the captain's single departing sentence. He began mumbling to himself. "It's a good thing we got that fish. If we'd lost it, he would have thrown me overboard, for sure. Neither one of us apologized. Wait 'til his wife sees, and smells, that ladle! Maybe we ought to have a commemoration engraved on its handle. I wonder what his wife will make of the condition of his hat and hair? Should I make arrangements to get some chum for tomorrow's trip?"

Bud got into his Jeep, started the engine and drove off, still mumbling to himself. "I will never understand that man, even if we fish together for the next thirty years!"

Chapter 16

Two Stinger Stories

Minnie Makes Her Move

"Women shouldn't be allowed to leave the dock." Ray was off on one of his harangues, trying to convince me the ocean was no place for females. I asked him to remember the many times we had had mixed charters, and we both agreed that the women always seemed to out-fish their male counterparts.

Ray backed off his hard-line attitude a bit by saying he was only referring to tuna fishing. "They just don't have the strength to handle those critters."

This conversation was brought on by our leaving for the tuna grounds right behind the *Stinger,* a beautifully set-up, 23-foot center console. Ray and I had exchanged good-wishes for the day's fishing with Mike and his wife, Minnie, before we left the town pier. I had to admit that Minnie, who was five feet tall and didn't weigh over 110 pounds, soaking wet, looked like she would have trouble hauling in a sea anchor, let alone a giant bluefin.

As the boats approached the end of the east jetty, side by side, I asked Mike to be sure to save us a good spot. "If we can, Cap" was his reply, as he hit the throttle and jumped *Stinger* to an easy 35 knots.

As he began preparing our hook baits, Ray mumbled something about Mike getting to the grounds in under 20 minutes. I set the throttle at cruising speed for our own hour and twenty-minute ride.

We were nearing the fleet when I noticed we were several microseconds north of our planned anchoring spot, so I changed course to the south'ard to compensate. When we cleared the big dragger anchored over the notch, I could see *Stinger*, set up about a football field further south. Mike waved and pointed to his starboard, indicating there was plenty of room for us on that side.

Half an hour later, after we had come taut on our anchor and set out Misty's hand lines, Ray began his chumming chores, and continued the conversation that had begun back at the harbor.

"Cap, do you really think Minnie would be able to haul in a giant? After all, most of them are eight or ten times her weight."

"Probably. She was tough enough to land Mike, wasn't she?" I answered, trying to end the conversation and concentrate on the job at hand.

Ray dropped some more chum chunks to port, then, almost in a whisper, said, "Check out *Stinger*. I think he's got one on!"

I looked to port and saw Minnie braced against the starboard quarter gunwale, with both hands bucking, as the handline slipped through them. The fish was headed toward Misty.

Mike released their anchor ball, cleared the other lines and started *Stinger,*'s engines. Minnie worked her way forward so the fish would be towing the boat easily straight ahead, allowing her to stop the slippage. Ray watched Minnie as she gained control of the fish, and acknowledged that she, at least, seemed to know what to do when she took a strike.

The gap between the two boats continued to close, so I called to Mike to let me know if he wanted me to drop my anchor ball. Minnie immediately interrupted with, "Don't bother, he's already cleared your anchor and headed for the deep water. We'll see you later." Mike added that they had decided, if they hooked-up today, it would be Minnie's fish, all the way, and he was just along to run the boat for her.

As they slid by, I glanced at Ray. His jaw was slack, his eyes were wide open, and for once, he had no comment. He just shrugged his shoulders and resumed his chumming.

Stinger's fish never moved more than half a mile from *Misty*. It seemed to prefer changing course, frequently, from north to south and back.

An hour went by, during which I noticed Ray keeping track of Minnie's struggle, and I knew he was just waiting to see Mike lend her a hand. He was itching for proof of his theory.

In another ten minutes, we could see some white water splashing around at *Stinger*'s bow. Minnie was braced in the port bow of the center console, with the handline bent over the gunwale for added control. Mike was in the stern, readying the cockpit harpoon. He moved forward with the harpoon in one hand and a milk crate, containing the line and tuna ball, in the other. Minnie straightened her back and gained another three or four feet of line. Mike raised the harpoon and drove it home.

The fight was over. All Ray and I heard was Minnie's jubilant one-word expression of victory, "YES!" as she pumped her fist in the air. Then she sat down in the helm-seat, like a queen on her throne, waiting for her subjects to kneel and give her the praises she had earned.

Mike dropped a tail-rope over the tail fins and proceeded to bleed the fish, while Minnie put the boat in gear and headed back to *Stinger*'s anchor ball, at idle speed. Minnie's smile could be seen across the water for the entire half-mile. As *Stinger* drew closer, it was easy to see the smile was not just joy and pride in what she had accomplished, it also radiated a quiet strength and satisfaction.

Ray had stopped chumming, He just stared at *Stinger* with a slack jawed expression of disbelief. We watched Mike haul his anchor and before he started for Green Harbor he swung close to *Misty*; I shouted "Great job, good going, Minnie!" She smiled again and said; "Thank you, I'm sure going to sleep tonight." Ray mumbled something that sounded somewhat like congratulations and then busied himself with some heavy chumming.

For the rest of the day, conversation aboard *Misty* was very sparse. Neither one of us mentioned what we had seen take place aboard *Stinger* until we were half way home and Ray was having his usual afternoon snack of a tuna-on-rye.

I couldn't help giving Ray a verbal jab in his male-chauvinist mind. I quietly reminded Ray that we had both been first-hand viewers as Minnie handlined a giant from hook-up to tail-rope with no help from Mike.

Being an eye witness to Minnie's feat seemed to have made very little impression on Ray, as he continued to wolf down the sandwich.

As he opened wide, he inserted both the last of the sandwich and his foot, into his mouth. I heard him munching and muttering something like, "women shouldn't be allowed on the sea", and, "the only contact they should have with tuna is when they open a can to make sandwiches for lunch".

The Day We Knit One

The date was 26 August 1978. This excerpt is from *Misty's* log for that date:

1st Hook-up 1130 hrs. - cut off under boat
2ndHook-up 1145 hrs. - spit hook
3rd Hook-up 1315 hrs. - tail-roped at 1400 hrs.
Fish wrapped up *Stinger*'s anchor line.
Weight 794 pounds whole, 745 pounds dressed
Length 107" - Girth 78" - Handlined.

This rather short entry tells when, what and how but it doesn't come close to telling the whole story.

My mate and I had no charter for this day so we decided to go meat fishing. The SW corner of Stellwagen Bank had had a good bite for the last two days and the odds were in our favor to make a days pay. We got a late start, but the word was the bite was lasting into the early afternoon. It was one of those rare days when it was just good to be on the water - not too hot, with a slight breeze producing just a hint of a ripple.

Misty came taught on her anchor around 1030 hrs. and I noticed we were about 100' south of *Stinger*. This triggered my memory so I told Bruce about the fish Minnie had taken on her own, and how I hoped it had helped to change Ray's outlook on female fishermen. Bruce gave me his usual you-gotta-be-kidding look and said "No way has anything changed the way Ray thinks about girls." This remark ended the conversation and we both turned-to.

We had two hits that resulted in subsequent misses. After the change of tide, the balloon farthest from the transom went under and imploded just as Bruce was starting to bring it in to check the hook bait. Bruce set the hook, "We've got this one, the third time's the charm."

I cleared the other lines and pulled the quick release to let the fish start towing *Misty*. When Bruce gained control, he said it was the first time he had ever taken a strike with the handline in-hand, and this one felt like a big fish.

The fish headed directly toward *Stinger*and before we could make a move, it had picked up *Stinger*'s deep handline and charged westward toward the deep water. I was grateful that Mike was an experienced tuna-man who could take-in a situation immediately. He quickly unclipped the tuna ball from the line our fish had snagged and watched as the entire line peeled from its milk carton.

The fish accelerated and soon *Misty* had swung around so it was being towed stern first. Everything seemed to be going right: We were free of any problem with other boats, the fish was working hard, and Bruce was keeping the status at quo with only one hand. I cleared the cockpit of all extraneous gear and we settled down for the struggle.

All of these were positive things and yet there was something negative gnawing at me. I couldn't put my finger on it and was about to express my apprehension, when Bruce looked at me and said "This fish is working hard but doesn't seem to be getting anywhere. Its as if he's working out on a treadmill." Just then I heard someone shouting from our bow's-end.

I turned around, and there was the *Stinger*, about 50 feet from us, with Mike in the bow holding his anchor line and seemingly pacing us without having his engine running. "That damn fish not only picked up my deep-line, but I think he's tail-wrapped on my anchor line as well. What do you want me to do, Cap?" I watched *Stinger* gradually closing the gap between the two boats.

"Let go your line and anchor ball and go back and jump on mine. That way you won't lose anymore good fishing time." Mike dropped the line and said, "Good idea, good luck." as Minnie started their engine.

Within the next five minutes, Mike's anchor ball moved down our port side and went aft of us to a position about three boat lengths beyond our stern. Bruce was able to gain line slowly. To a casual observer it must have looked as if *Misty* was being towed stern-to by a 40" tuna ball running amuck!

While Bruce gained line, I coiled it back into its basket, and noticed the distance to *Stinger's* anchor ball was diminishing and the angle to the fish seemed to become shallower. Bruce was shaking his head with a bewildered expression on his face, "I can't figure it out, Cap. The fish is tail-wrapped; he's working himself toward the surface, and we're gaining on *Stinger's* anchor ball."

I had coiled all the pot-warp into the basket and Bruce had started retrieving the Sampson cord, when he paused and said the fish had just become a dead weight and had given up the struggle. He hauled back until he could see the bitter end of the Sampson cord wrapped around both the upper and lower parts of the caudal fin. He could see no evidence of the 30' mono leader.

Suddenly the fish was belly-up next to *Stinger's* anchor ball, feebly trying to swim away from its antagonists. The exhausted fish, only a boat length away, looked as if it was wrapped in a net. Bruce retrieved the last few feet of line, tail-wrapped the fish and secured the line to a cleat. I put *Misty* in idle to plane the fish aft of the stern for Bruce to bleed. "Cap, take it out of gear." I did so and went aft to see what he was pointing at.

We could see a line leading down from his left pectoral that had been pinned to his body by the "net." I grabbed a gaff and in short order we had 200' of anchor line, 20' of 5/8 inch chain and what looked like a brand new anchor lying on the cockpit sole.

The rest of *Stinger's* anchor warp along with Mike's deep-line was woven around the fish. I checked the time: Only 40 minutes since we hooked up.

Bruce moved the tail rope to the starboard cleat and tied a line around the part of *Stinger's* anchor line holding the tuna's mouth almost completely shut. With this set up, we started to free our captive from its self-imposed prison.

After 20 minutes of leaning over the gunwale, one of us rolling the prisoner while the other pulled at the "net," we had only gained another 40' of *Stinger's* anchor warp. When we straightened up to clear our heads and work out the kinks in our backs, Bruce took out his knife and ran his thumb across the blade. "My blade's real sharp, Cap; how about using it?"

"Can't do that. I'm not going to return Mike's gear in a fish box full of six foot sections." Bruce nodded assent, put away his knife and we returned to our work.

When the last coil slipped free of the gill-plates the critter came alive and began slapping the hull with its tail. Bruce moved the tail rope to the starboard quarter, cleated it off and began raking the gills with the cockpit harpoon as I slipped *Misty* into idle to facilitate the bleeding.

The mate and I spent the next twenty minutes, starting with the anchor ball, straightening and then coiling the warp into a fish box, topped it off with the chain and the brand new anchor. I climbed to the bridge, leaving the coiling of Mike's deep-line, the line that started our captive's imprisonment, to the mate.

I could hear Bruce mumbling to himself repeatedly - "Knit one, purl two; knit one, purl two." I looked back at the tuna fleet; it was hull down, and I realized we had been drifting and working ourselves to the west ever since the hook-up.

I called Mike on the working channel, told him we had the fish and that all his gear was coiled in a fish box ready for transfer, and would he mind hauling my gear and bring it to our harbor, since we were already half way to port.

Mike came back with congratulations, saying he would haul our gear, and he wanting to know how and why *Stinger* and his anchor ball had been pulled to *Misty's* bow? I answered all would be revealed when we swapped anchors in Green Harbor. Bruce rigged the fish for towing head-first and we headed for the barn.

I looked at my watch. "Hey, Bruce, this has got to be a first; it took us over twice as long to free that critter from his 'net,' than it did for you to handline him all the way to the tail rope."

Chapter 17

Three main methods — Rod & Reel – Handline – Harpoon

Rod & Reel

The last two or three years of the '60s saw the beginning of a strong interest in angling for bluefin. The challenge of their raw power and stamina alone was enough to intrigue recreational anglers. The regulations for recreational angling put forth by the IGFA (International Game Fish Association) made the taking of bluefin by rod and reel a proud accomplishment. Those regulations included:

- 130 lb. test line – maximum
- 30' double line – maximum
- 15' leader – maximum
- Angler must take strike, set hook and fight fish to leader — unassisted.
- Crew can only help by "wiring" fish to boat with leader only.
- Must use only flying gaff and tail-rope.

At this time, in the Cape Cod and Massachusetts Bay areas, the term "Giant," as applied to bluefin tuna, designated a fish of 600 pounds or more. When the NMFS (National Marine Fisheries Service) began regulating the tuna fishery, they decided a "Giant" was any bluefin over 300 pounds. That designation was considered ridiculous by most of the tuna fishermen working Massachusetts' waters. During the '70s, I remember hearing of only two or three fish being brought to port that weighted less than 600 pounds.

When the Japanese appetite for bluefin created a growing commercial market in 1976, all but a few "sportsman anglers" put the IGFA regulations aside. Those claiming to be recreational-fishermen were still selling their catch to "pay their boating expenses." If you intend to fish for tuna you must obtain a federal permit – before even wetting a line – which, of course, means you are considered commercial, and subject to all of the NMFS regulations.

The commercial market was also the impetus for major changes in the equipment used by rod and reelers. As prices rose, so did the strength of the running line. It didn't take long before most everyone was using lines of 200-pound test, and in some cases even 250-pound test. The use of the stronger lines lowered the yards/capacity of the reels causing a trade-off dilemma for many of the captains.

The IGFA regulations were given the deep six. After the 130-pound test line, the next thing to go was the flying gaff, which was quickly replaced with the much more efficient cockpit harpoon. The double line and leaders increased in both length and strength.

As president of the Green Harbor Tuna Club, I urged the members to offer any boat, participating in their tournaments, a choice of fishing under the IGFA rules or fishing in an alternate unlimited category – whereupon duplicate prizes would be awarded – but the skippers had to make their choice at sign-up, prior to the tournament. Many other tuna clubs offered similar style tournaments

If the government regulations were permitting a catch of two fish a day, and a skipper wished to come up with a double fee, he was allowed to fish both IGFA and unlimited gear — the only caveat being that he had to report which method he was using for each catch, at the moment of hook-up.

Throughout the '70s and '80s, the reels of choice were the Penn Senator 14/0 and 16/0 big game reels — dubbed the "Black-Beauties." The 16/0 Penn Senator had a capacity of 1600 yards of 130-pound test Dacron; a capacity that translates into a little over 3/4 mile. (Although if anyone allows a fish to get that far away, they could stand some basic instruction about the use of a drag system, and aside from that, they had better be hooked to a tuna with an overpowering death-wish. Even then, their chance of boating the fish is about equal to winning the lottery.)

Rod & reelers are split between those who prefer trolling and those who favor chumming. I can't recommend one method over the other, but the split points up the difference that takes place in every fishery. An old timer once told me that there were only two ways to catch fish: "You either go where *they* are, or you can stay still and attract them to where *you* are."

Trolling is essentially taking the bait to the fish and displaying it enticingly to elicit a strike. Chumming is creating a chum stream that will attract the fish to the bait and, hopefully have it engulf the chunk or whole bait (alive or dead) with the hook in it. Either method boils down to the same kind of fight — even though purists will always claim that the best way to take a tuna is by rod & reel, from a fighting chair.

Handline

Capt. Donald Hebert *(Chapter 14)* is primarily responsible for the development of the tuna handline and the most effective way to use it to capture these powerful fish. He designed and refined the gear that has become the standard for this fishery.

The basic ingredients used for a tuna handline consists of a tuna ball (a buoy), 300 feet of pot warp, 50 to 100 feet of Sampson cord, 30 feet of leader and a tuna hook. The handline is set-up by forming a loop in one end of the pot warp and placing it next to a milk-carton or laundry style basket. Coil the warp into the basket and attach the Sampson cord to it; then coil that into the basket, on top of the warp, followed by the leader and hook. The tuna ball is either secured directly onto the loop next to the basket, or it can have a short pigtail line with a swordfish clip to snap onto the loop next to the basket. (I always had short pigtail lines and swordfish clips on my tuna balls because of the versatility it provided; plus they could easily hang anywhere, out of the way, until needed.)

Serious handliners were known to use at least six of these set-ups, four for deployment aft of the transom, and two hanging straight down amidships. In addition to the six tuna baskets, we soon learned to prepare one more set-up, with just the warp and tuna ball. We used a swordfish clip on the bitter end so we could make a quick connection to the loop and tuna-ball-end of any handline, when it first became hooked-up. This "safety line" added another 300′ of line for the angler to work, incase the quarry "screamed" and took all of the first handline into the water. (Two football fields of length between angler and fish is still do-able when handlining.)

The cost of the gear then for six handlines was about $600, opposed to the cost of just one tuna rod and reel, at $1,000. (Today, a Penn International Two-Speed Reel, alone, goes for more than a grand.)

1976 was a year of tremendous change — mainly because of the sudden rise in value of bluefin tuna in the Japanese market, which in turn changed the way fishermen viewed the emerging fishery. If a recreational boat owner could capture one or two fish in a season, those fish could theoretically pay for the slip fee, as well as the cost of fuel for the year. This fact alone attracted hundreds of new "commercial" fishermen, to take

Handlining set-up — a basketful of Sampson cord and accessories

advantage of the free federal permits.

By 1978, the average fish was worth over $1,000, so it didn't take long for fishermen to do the math and decide to switch to handlines.

Capt. Donald Hebert and I engaged in many arguments during 1976 and 1977, always about the same subject. I held a firm position that handlining was taking unfair advantage of the fish (I was still a purest at the time). He would counter by saying, "If an experienced rod and reeler has ten hook-ups and successfully lands even three fish, he's considered a highliner. Give those same ten hook-ups to me, and if I don't land at least seven of those fish, I'll be totally pissed-off." He would always end the discussion with the same irrefutable statement, "Don't knock it 'til you've done it."

Don had a great way of making his point; he offered to take me with him as an observer to get some first hand knowledge. I decided to take him up on the offer by saying, "OK, but it won't change the facts. It takes too much advantage of the fish."

Don anchored the *White Lady* just off the steep drop-off, on the SW corner of the Bank, at 0445 the next morning. Shortly after we fetched up on the anchor, as the sky was just starting to show the beginning of false dawn, one of the lines we had just deployed went off with the snap of its breaker string.

Don, with a quiet, matter-of-fact tone said, "We're on," as he set the hook. I pulled the quick release on the anchor ball and watched the crew clear the other lines. I turned my attention to the Captain, who was holding the line with his right hand and motioning for me to come aft with his left.

He urgently said: "Hold this for me a minute, will ya?" as he handed the hook-up to me.

From that instant on, handlining has been my favorite way of engaging bluefin in battle. It is the classic "David and Goliath" struggle; a basic one-on-one tug-of-war. It's you on one end and the fish on the other, with the transom as the line you'd better not cross, or else you lose! There is one saving grace that cuts the angler some slack — the transom is not an unmovable line drawn on the water; it moves as the boat is being towed, and as long as the angler is not giving the fish any line, the struggle remains in neutral.

Here is where the size of the vessel can make a big difference in the capture. A large vessel is hard to tow backwards and therefore the fish has to use more energy; but the angler will have a more difficult time gaining line. A smaller vessel won't tire the fish as much; but the angler will be able to pull the boat to the fish. It's a trade off that should be taken into account. *(See Chapter 21)*

Think about this: A rod & reeler has many mechanical advantages. The bent-butt makes it easier for him to put a curve in the rod, and keep it in. That curve imparts kinetic energy that puts more pressure on the fish. He can also hike himself into the air and use his own weight against the fish; by leaning back and sitting down again he adds to the curve, thereby giving him more leverage and placing more pressure on the fish.

The drag system puts the brakes on the fish. The angler can even fine-tune the drag by using his thumbs on the sides of the spool. The ratio of the spool to the cranking handle aids the angler when he is in a grind-it-out-fight with a giant. (Two speed reels, when in high gear, also give the angler the ability to retrieve line faster when a fish charges the boat.)

All this, and I haven't even mentioned the captain's use of the boat. Maneuvering the boat to counter the actions of the fish makes it the most important fishing "tool" for eroding the prey's stamina.

The only advantage a handliner can use during a confrontation with a giant is to take a turn over the gunwale with the line; doing this will double his holding power, while giving him a chance to rest and get his second wind. The problem is, taking a turn over the gunwale negates the ability to gain line.

Catching a tuna by handline is almost always quicker than using rod and reel. The reason is in the strength of the tackle being used. The weakest part of any tackle set-up should be the leader. In the early years of handlining, (1976 thru 1978) we were using seven-strand cable with a breaking strength of 465 pounds. It wasn't necessary to darken the leader, or even try to hide the hook in the bait. There were so many giants around that the competition for a free lunch was intense, and they'd "Take a bite out of ANY crime" offered them.

During the '70s, despite being offered plenty to eat, they had to compete for their daily sustenance with what seemed to be an overpopulation of the species. Hunger will make any species less cautious and less picky about what they ingest.

Tuna are at the top of the fish ladder in strength, speed, agility, stamina and intelligence. I am convinced they can also communicate at a higher level than just conveying warning signals when danger is near, finding their way when they migrate, or working together when food must be corralled. It seemed apparent that they could even spread the word that it was unhealthy to grab a snack when it is attached to something leading to the surface. In this fishery, any new kind of tackle or method of fishing will last only a year or two before the tuna learn how to avoid or out smart it.

By 1979, cable was "out" and single-strand wire was "in". Coffee colored Malin wire, (everybody called it piano-wire), usually with a breaking strength of 325 lbs, was the hot new item. Each succeeding year, however, we found it necessary to use thinner, less visible, piano-leaders. By 1984, most all of the handliners were having trouble hooking up, even when using 125 lb. test Malin, which, of course, the fish were quite often able to break.

Fishermen have a highly developed form of communication and an ability to pick up on (or should I say steal) new ideas and methods from each other. A few tuna men began using monofilament leaders with some success, and almost over night the market for Malin wire ended. The fishery had made another major move. Mono was again the way to go. But, the fish were soon avoiding even 250 lb. test mono. Each year the ability of the fish to "recognize" and avoid mono, even at reduced-strength, became more evident.

Rod & Reel — Again?

The end of the '80s saw another change taking place; it was a gradual shift from handlining back to rod and reel. This time the fighting chair did not factor into the fight. In the early '90s, everyone in the tackle business knew major changes were afoot. The demand for both new and used unlimited tuna rods and Penn International 130 & 80 Reels quickly scoffed up all existing supplies.

Tuna were bringing as much as $14 to $20 per pound. (Some individual fish were sold for as much as $20,000!) A cost of five grand to make the switch back to rod & reel was not prohibitive (at least for fishermen who knew the how, when and where of tuna taking, plus maybe a few who were just damn lucky.) The switch over was rumored as another reason for the rise in the divorce rate in some coastal communities.

The new method involved a flush mounted vertical rod holder with a swivel base. When a hook-up occurs and the hook is set, the crew ignores that rod and clears all other lines. Next, a crewmember stands next to the hooked-up rod and cranks the tip over, until it almost reaches the surface. He waits for the rod's kinetic energy to dissipate as the rod gradually straightens; then he cranks the rod over again. This cycle is repeated, again and again, until the fish is literally winched into cockpit-harpoon range. (I know this is a rather simplistic explanation of how it was done, but it covers the basic strategy.) As with any tuna fishing technique, the guy who runs the boat and makes the decisions is the determining factor in a successful capture.

Harpoon

Only two things are involved when a harpoon is the weapon of choice, and only one of them is "fishing" — the other is "hunting." Up to the point where you actually stick the fish, you are engaged in seeking out, tracking, and positioning yourself for a shot at the prey. This activity is akin to that of a deer hunter, from the first sight of the prey to the pull of the trigger.

Once a fish has been stuck the hunting is over and the game becomes one of fishing. The harpoon basket is very similar to the handlining basket — a tuna ball, attached to 300′ of pot warp, tied to 100′ of Sampson cord — but hooked to a bridled tuna dart instead of a leader. The dart is placed on the end of a 16″ or 18″ shank that is fixed to the end of the "stick." Sticks vary in length to accommodate the height of the thrower, as well

Capt. Rog prepares to harpoon a fish that's invisible to the camera

as the distance from the water to the stand, at the forward end of the pulpit.

Throwing-harpoons can be anywhere from 16′ to 20′ in length. An early '70's harpoon was usually made from a length of round ash stairwell railing, because it held its shape. Other woods were prone to bowing, which rendered them useless when trying to make an accurate throw. A well-made stick must also be weighted at the shank end to increase accuracy, and add penetrating power to the dart. Most stick-men would accomplish this by wrapping lead sheathing (the same as that used by carpenters on roofs around chimneys) around the harpoon's business end.

By the end of the decade, the wooden sticks had been replaced by aluminum tubing with the added weight being a slug of lead inside the shank end.

The up-close and personal distance necessary for a successful "shot" at a bluefin is what differentiates a harpooner from a hunter. A distance of thirty feet has a very low percentage rate of "hits," and a twenty-foot throw, even by an experienced harpooner, might come close to a 50/50 chance of reaching the target. When deer hunting, a fifty-yard shot has a very low percentage, and a twenty- yard shot is considered to be within the 50/50 range of success. The mathematical equation is that the harpooner must be three times closer than the hunter before attempting a throw. Unless the pulpit stand is within 20 feet of the "stickee," my advice would always be, "Don't even think about it."

Some of a tuna man's best days are the ones he spends in the tower or crow's nest, looking for signs of fish cruising on or near the surface. A well-equipped crow's nest has a full set of controls, a compass, radio and an intercom to the pulpit. (After a few hours of constant searching the eyes can blur and the head ache, but if the fish show, the rush of adrenaline clears both – very quickly.)

The man in the crow's nest (the skipper) has complete control of the boat's speed, direction and maneuvers. He is also responsible for placing the boat behind, and close enough to the pod, to afford the harpooner a chance at a good clean shot.

Once a pod of tuna is spotted "pushing" (usually a group of two, three, or four fish, swimming on or near the surface, in formation, and on a specific course), the general procedure is to turn away from the fish and come about, to a position that is behind and on the same track as the fish.

At this point the skipper takes note of their course and sets the throttle so the boats speed is just a bit faster than that of the prey. You should be about 1/2 NM or more behind the pod. This distance will give the fish time to get used to the sound of your engine; the steady purr of the engine can mesmerize the pod so your approach doesn't alarm them. From here on, what ever you do, do **not** touch the throttle! The slightest change in RPMs can alert the pod to the danger. Once the fish are alerted the stalker might as well "fahgedabowdit."

The typical behavior of a "pushing" pod is to stay on course, periodically baring their backs before diving, leaving only a "V" shaped wake (even that may disappear if they go deep enough.) Soon, the wake will show again as their dorsal fins and tails come clear of the surface, and the cycle repeats. With each cycle, you should be closer, and better able to judge the correct time for the stick man to move to the pulpit and prepare for the sticking.

From here on, the pressure is on the harpooner. He must pick one fish in the pod as his target, and narrow his concentration to that one fish only. (The best chance of success is to pick the trailing fish, just like our Minutemen would pick off the last British soldier in a column). Nothing else matters, and the sticker must really-want-that-fish! He must determine when conditions are right to afford him the best chance for a shot. As a hunter, he cannot afford to freeze when it's time to "pull the trigger".

A good hunter soon learns to lead a moving target, while he remains completely still and quiet. A harpooner not only has to lead his moving target, he has to do it standing on a moving platform; one that is not only moving forward, but going up and down, and subject to sporadic side-to-side pitches as well. It's no wonder he has to get within twenty feet for a 50/50 chance of success!

There is really no normal condition for sticking; with all the variables listed above, it is a wonder that tuna can be harpooned at all. Believe me, a good stick-man is a rare and wonderful being, well worth whatever cut of the proceeds he gets.

The rule of thumb for leading the target is to aim for a point just ahead of the nose. Under "normal conditions" (did I just say that?), this amount of lead should put the dart's point of entry just aft of the gill plates. This scenario assumes the fish is at the top of his cycle, and on or very close to the surface. If a fish is 10, 5 or even 4 feet under water, he is not where he appears to be. A little thing called refraction comes into play; the bending of light rays as they enter the water causes a visual distortion, making the fish look farther ahead, or to the side than it really is. If you stop to calculate all the factors, you will probably freeze and not make the shot. The best advice: "Don't hesitate. Concentrate." Focus completely on your chosen target and give it hell. The window of opportunity is open for only an instant, and if you stop to think, you'll surely miss it.

Becoming one with the targeted fish is paramount. I once tracked a three-fish pod, and when they came up about 100′ ahead, I picked the trailing fish as my target. As they went down, I made my move to the stand. I watched for the "V" wake, between and just behind the other two, and unlashed the harpoon. Raising it to vertical with the dart just above the surface, I cocked my arm as my target began to slice the surface, slightly ahead of the stand. I had the perfect shot.

Just then, the fish on the right flashed a little of its white belly. It was just enough to attract my eye for a split second and break my concentration. In that instant, my target exploded into a tower of white water and was gone! My disappointment was the direct result of letting myself be distracted by something I should have ignored. (On land, a glimpse of white belly attracts my eye, too — and in most cases, should never be ignored.)

In the '90s, the increased pressure on the fish from the proliferation of tuna boats, and the use of airplanes for spotting had a traumatic effect on the fish. They became much more wary of the changes to their environment. They learned not to stay on the surface for long, when they did show themselves, and it became very rare to see them "pushing". This is another example of their ability to communicate and make adjustments necessary to their survival. If they didn't get hungry and become reckless in their pursuit of food, the catch ratio would continually diminish.

Harpooning changed from spotting and tracking-down, to spotting and charging-at. The challenge became; can the boat get off a shot before the fish becomes aware of its approach? The ideal situation is to find a school of tuna that are rolling around, feeding heavily on baitfish, small bluefish, sand eels, etc, and enjoying the chance to pig-out. This active feeding lowers their normal awareness of encroaching danger.

I once watched a stick boat working a large school of feeding bluefin. I estimated the average fish to weigh about 500 lbs. each. There were three men aboard the boat; the skipper, a highliner, was in the crow's nest running the show, the stick man was on the stand, and the third man was in the cockpit with a clipboard and pencil. (The boat had been called to the feeding fish by a circling spotter plane).

The foredeck was crowed with tuna baskets, each with its own tuna ball attached. I counted six hi-flyers set in racks and stacked against the windshield. One harpoon was tied crossways on the stand and there were two spare harpoons in holsters on each side of the pulpit. This was a serious operation.

The man in the crows-nest would charge a fish on the edge of the school; the man on the pulpit would stick it, and the running line would quickly leave one of the baskets. There was no attempt to set the hook or even try at controlling the running line. Shortly after the tuna ball was pulled overboard and into the water, one of the hi-flyers was yanked from its rack and went overboard, following the ball.

The stick-man retrieved the harpoon (via a safety line), reloaded it with a new dart and the next running line, while the skipper, from the crows-nest, turned the boat to charge another fish.

This scenario was repeated five more times. Within a half hour, all the baskets were empty, the tuna balls were in the water and all six hi-flyers were gone from the rack.

All three men gathered in the cockpit, and it was then that I noticed each hi-flyer had a numbered flag. The man with the clipboard was now in charge. It had been his job to keep track of the whereabouts of each fish, and to know the order in which they had been stuck.

The last hi-flyer to be yanked overboard was still heading east at a good pace. I scanned the area and noticed the first two hi-flyers were already stationary, next to their slowly turning tuna balls. The crew went to work, very methodically, starting with the first fish and proceeding down the list in the order of their sticking, and ultimate demise.

Three hours later, the three-man crew had bled and boated six tuna, weighing an approximate total of 3000 pounds. The rule of thumb for loss of weight, from whole fish to dressed fish, is between 22 and 25 percent, making this day's haul about 2300 pounds of dressed weight. At the going rate of $12 per pound, that would bring $27,600. Split five ways, including the three-man crew, the spotter-plane pilot, and the boat, each would average $5520…not a bad day's pay!

Priorities & Styles

These three basic methods of taking tuna are very different in their approach, and of course, the equipment varies widely; but the choice of methods is up to the skipper and his priorities. The styles applied to each method are as numerous as the crews pursuing the mighty tuna, but those styles are greatly affected by the stamina and intelligence of the prey.

The ingenuity and know-how of the fisherman often determines the outcome of the struggle. — Does he win or does he fall prey to the prey?

Chapter 18

What a Day a Difference Makes

It was August of 1976. Ray, my mate, and I were looking forward to the next day — one where we could hang out with friends and family — a day off!

We were finishing off 15 straight days of charters. Ray and I were both wound up so tight we were ready to use each other as terminal tackle. What we needed was a day off to try to make some sort of an attitude adjustment. I had been thinking about what to do with my free time, when the mate broke into my thoughts with, "Cap, I got a great idea. Lets go fishing tomorrow."

Rationalization reared its ugly head, and caused a tug-of-war in mine: "I need to mow the lawn, but I haven't wet a line for myself in weeks. I should do some maintenance on the engine, but the blues are bigger than I've seen in years. The weather is perfect and time off is a time to enjoy one's self, right? When in Rome . . . There is nothing like a busman's holiday."

When I arrived the next morning, the mate had made all preparations for getting under way. Sitting on the transom, with his 11′ surf-stick, was "Sandy Surf Rat." Sandy, at age nineteen, had already gained a considerable reputation as a fisherman who knew his way around the sand and suds. "Can I go along Captain?" I saw Ray shrug and smile. "OK, but you have to use that weapon of yours only from the pulpit. Any thing that long has got to be isolated, so it can't cause any harm to man or beast!"

An hour and a half later we began one of those vivid days that will always remain a benchmark in my mind. We started in 30′ of water, between the sand bars off Peaked Hill on the backside of Cape Cod, about three miles below the Coast Guard Beach.

The bluefish were top-to-bottom and wall-to- wall between the bars, and they were in a feeding frenzy.

After assigning Ray to the cockpit, I sent Sandy to the pulpit. This put him 13 feet ahead of the bow and assured both Ray and me that we were out of harm's way. I began climbing to the bridge for a better view of the proceedings. Both Ray and Sandy had hooked-up before I reached the top rung. I reversed my steps and before I reached the cockpit sole, they were both yelling for the gaff. It was time for a procedural summit, and since I was the captain of this democratically run vessel, with 100% of the vote, I declared that each angler had to take care of his own catch. I grabbed my light spinning rod and climbed to the bridge to join in on the fun.

These fish were a real challenge on light tackle. The small members of the school were 15 or 16 pounders, but some of them ranged up to 22 or 23 pounds. My personal memory of this day is that I boated 46 pounds of bluefish with a cast and a half;

Misty heads out for a "busman's holiday" with pulpit fully extended.

at least that is the way I like to tell it. With my first cast I hooked and landed the biggest blue I had ever caught. I had to weigh it right away; it pulled the scale to an even 23 pounds. I placed it in a fish box and returned to the bridge. I heaved the plug to the roiling water and before it splashed down another blue cleared the surface and engulfed the plug in mid-air. (Half a cast?) I swung it aboard; it looked like a twin to my first catch. Its weight? — 23 and 1/2 pounds. Total weight boated for that cast and a half came to 46 1/2 pounds. Five or six of these beauties would fill a fish box to overflowing.

That was some of the most exciting and satisfying fishing I had ever done, but it couldn't come close to the events that would take place on the rest of the trip.

At the end of the first hour, I was arm weary and had decided I would get one more blue and then relax and enjoy the beautiful day nature had provided.

Before ascending the bridge ladder to make my final cast I paused to watch Sandy's plug darting and spitting its way toward the starboard side, amidships. When it was about five feet from the hull there was a violent explosion of water as a five hundred pound bluefin tuna engulfed his plug and set off toward the deeper water beyond the outer sand bar. Neither Sandy nor Ray had seen the explosion. Sandy was holding on to his surf rod with both hands and the expression on his face was somewhere between startled and quizzical.

When I reached the bridge, Sandy was pointing to starboard with his left hand, while holding the rod in a death grip with his right, "That way, that way, that way!" I dropped *Misty* into gear, put the throttle to the max and headed in the direction Sandy was pointing.

"What the hell is going on?" Ray screamed from the cockpit. I looked aft; skipping along the surface with his mouth wide open was a bluefish with a "this is not one of my better days" look in his eyes. Ray quickly boated the fish and scrambled to the bridge.

"What the hell is going on?" Ray repeated. I said, "Sandy has a tuna on and he's convinced he can take him with his surf outfit. Looks to me like the fish is the *taker* and Sandy is the *takee*." Ray broke into one of his broad grins: "Sandy only uses 16-pound test; that's going to be like trying to stop a runaway freight train by putting a penny on the track."

The bend in Sandy's rod began to straighten and he signaled for me to slow down. I throttled back and as our momentum slowed Sandy began to gain line. After several minutes *Misty* had come to a complete stop, Sandy's spool was a little more than half full and the line was straight up and down. He looked up at the bridge, shrugged his shoulders and gingerly began to lift the tip of his surf stick. The tip of the rod went into the water to the second guide as Sandy pointed out to sea, "That way, that way, that way!!!"

Off we went again, only this time Ray and I were doing a lousy job of trying not to laugh. Sandy again had the butt in his crotch, holding the fore-grip with both hands. He glanced over his shoulder at us, holding each other up, and exclaimed. "What are you guys laughing about? Help me out here, this is serious business. I'm going to get this big guy." Another ten or twelve minutes went by and the fish again slowed his pace.

I throttled down and took *Misty* out of gear. Sandy was again gaining line but this time there was a difference: The angle of his line to the fish was now about thirty degrees, much less than the first time the fish had slowed. The fish seemed to be swimming unconcernedly; as if he was unaware he was hooked. *Misty* came to a stop. Sandy had gained almost all of his line; the spool looked full and the line was once again vertical. He bent over the bucket railing and stared into the water. "I see him, he's right here, only five feet down. The son-of-a-gun is looking right at me. What do I do now?" Sandy looked up at the bridge and repeated his question. Ray somehow managed a sober expression and said, "Hold him right there until I get the gaff,"

Sandy looked back at his quarry and then put just a slight

amount of lift into his rod. With this tiny tug on the plug, Mr. Bluefin had had enough of playing games. A few flicks of his tail and he was gone.

The resulting splash turned the water under the pulpit white and thoroughly soaked Sandy. In that instant his expression changed from wonderment to complete disappointment, and as he reeled in the last few feet of his line, he ended the episode by admonishing Ray: "I might have caught him if you had been a little quicker with the gaff."

I checked the time and the distance off shore. We were now four miles from our starting point. Sandy had been hooked-up for almost half an hour and the depth had gone from thirty feet to well over four hundred.

Sandy slowly sulked his soaked self off the pulpit and we decided to call it a day. Sandy stuffed his surf rod in a rod-holder sat down on the foredeck, leaning against the wind-shield, so the sun and wind would dry him off. I headed *Misty* back toward Green Harbor.

When we reached the Race Point buoy, off the tip of the Cape, the surface of the whole area was alive with bluefish in a feeding frenzy, much the same as we had seen earlier while fishing the backside, below the CG beach.

Sandy looked up and asked if he could get one more blue? I answered by throttling down and bringing *Misty* to a stop. He moved to the pulpit and had a fish on with the first cast.

Ray poked me in the ribs and pointed to a fresh humpback whale "footprint" off our starboard side. "If he comes up again he should be just under Sandy's feet. Don't say anything, let's see if my calculations are accurate." A minute went by and we could see the long pectoral fin coming up about thirty feet to the right of the end of the pulpit. First the jaw and then the blow-hole appeared under Sandy's feet.

"Phwoooossshhh" and Sandy was soaked for the second time in under an hour, only this time the water had a distinct odor of very bad "morning-breath." The blow from a whale is often worse than the smell of cod excrement. He reeled the blue in as far as the fish would allow, cut the line, giving it its freedom, and said: "Okay, I surrender. This day is going down the tubes fast. Can we go home now?"

He sloshed back to the bow, and returned to his position on the foredeck to dry out. Both Ray and I were glad we were on the bridge, well above the prevailing breeze for the trip back to harbor.

Back at the slip, a still odorous Sandy thanked Ray and me for the "different" day we had enjoyed. As he walked up the ramp, we could hear him mumbling something about hoping a long hot shower would remove the stench, if and when his mother would let him in the house.

Ray, who always manages to have the last say, said, "Don't forget, it's not what's going down the tubes that counts, it's what's coming out of the tubes that can ruin your day!"

Chapter 19

Double Barrels & Hard Of Hearing

"Hey Cap, that's the third hook-up in an hour. I hope he gets him this time." Sam and I were anchored on the SW corner of Stellwagen Bank on our favorite LORAN numbers. I made a comment about the luck of the Irish. Owen O'Brien, the skipper of the *Double Oh* had already hooked and dropped two fish, and it was only 0715.

This is the sequence of the strange but inevitable events that took place that morning.

We had pulled into the fleet at 0600 and anchored about 50 yards south of *Double Oh.* As Misty settled on its anchor, another boat pulled into the fleet and anchored close behind Owen. I heard him yell something about it being a little too close astern. Hearing no reply, he shrugged his massive shoulders and returned to his "chopping and plopping."

We were busy setting out our lines when the first audible "snap" was heard coming from Owen's boat. He grabbed the line, set the hook and the mate cleared the rest of the lines, while the fish pulled the *Double Oh* toward the newcomer, directly astern. Owen was asking the skipper, with his usual calm and measured tones, to let go his anchor ball. There being no response, he added a few decibels to his voice and again made his request. Suddenly, as the two boats drew closer to each other, the fish broke off and Owen disgustedly threw the limp line onto the cockpit sole.

I glanced at my watch; it was only 0622.

On his way back to his anchor ball, Owen swung by my starboard side. "Sorry you lost him Cap. What's with that guy anyway?"

"He must be hard of hearing. If it happens again I'll make sure he hears me. All you have to do with his type is to first get his attention and then express yourself in no uncertain terms."

Twenty minutes later we again heard that wonderful "snap" as *Double Oh* had its second hook-up. This time you could have heard Owen if you were surf fishing at Race Point, eight miles to the south'ard. "Hey, Cap! How about giving me some help? Drop your ball and give me a chance to catch this guy. DROP YOUR BALL, DAMNIT."

The newcomer looked up, cupped his hand to his ear and feigned incomprehension, as the two boats were again drawing together. The fish wrapped its self around the guy's anchor line and before Owen could either unwrap it or cut the line, the fish was able to abrade the leader and break off.

The one-way conversation ended abruptly and once again the *Double Oh* returned to its anchor ball.

As he passed us again, Owen said, "He heard me this time but I still haven't gotten his attention. The next time I'll get his attention first." After looking at his flushed face with its slitted eyes and tightened lips, I thought better of asking him how he was going to accomplish that task. I muttered something about the third time being the charm and good luck.

Another half hour went by. I continued to chum while, in my mind, there was no doubt that Owen would get another hook-up. As I was mulling this premise over, it was suddenly confirmed, as again there was the tell-tail breaker string "snap."

Both Sam and I stopped our routines and turned our attention to the activity on *Double Oh*. Owen set the hook and immediately took a turn over the gunnel. As the mate was clearing the other lines, I noticed Owen hadn't pulled his quick release. Apparently he had decided to take this fish very quickly and without any fanfare.

As soon as the other lines were coiled in their baskets, he passed the hooked-up line to the mate and disappeared into the cabin. By the time Sam had asked me what I thought the skipper was doing down below, he reappeared with a double-barreled shotgun and placed it on the transom gunnel.

There was no shouting this time. Owen curled his tongue and produced a prodigious whistle that turned every head on all of the boats in the fleet, including that of the newcomer. Having gained the skipper's attention, Owen next used both arms with forefingers extended, to jab at the newcomer forcefully, and then pointedly pointed to the weapon. He then calmly took the line from the mate.

There was immediate action by those on the newcomers boat; lines retrieved, engine started, and the anchor ball released. The skipper might be hard of hearing but it was apparent that his eyesight was not at all impaired. He stared at the gun and then quietly backed away from Owen's boat.

Owen took a turn around his waist, (This is a no-no unless you are the size of, and possess the strength of, this man) and leaned into the fish as if defying it to take out any more line. The mate was busying himself preparing the harpoon and making ready the tail rope.

The situation was now this: The anchor was not about to drag, the fish was not going to give in, and Owen was certainly not allowing it even one more inch. As the fish struggled, you could see the *Double Oh* surge back and forth while its anchor ball, acting as a shock absorber, bobbed with the motion of the boat.

Equal opposing forces tend to remain in balance as long as there is no change in attitude or power, and it was obvious that Owen was not about to change his. Several minutes passed and then the fish charged the *Double Oh.*

The Captain retrieved the handline as fast as possible, trying to keep pressure on the quarry, and once again the newcomer's ball began approaching his transom. One obscene word from Owen and it was obvious, for the third time that morning a fish had taken a turn around the newcomer's anchor warp.

When the ball reached the transom, Owen deftly flipped the line up and around the ball, freeing it, and then continued working the fish. Another five minutes and the fish was tail-roped. Only then did he start his engine and pull his quick release so he could leave the fleet and properly bleed his captive.

He returned a half hour later and went directly to the newcomer's boat, pulled alongside and engaged the skipper in serious conversation. I was unable to hear what was being said, but the dialog seemed to be conducted in a very calm manner. There was very little gesturing.

After stowing all his gear he hauled the fish aboard and iced it down, and then swung by me on his way home. "Hope I never have to take another fish while I'm on my anchor; it ain't easy Cap." Seeing the expression of curiosity on my face, he added, "I explained some of the basic courtesies that take place among tuna fishermen here in the fleet. It's funny how much a person's hearing can improve once you get their attention. I have a feeling he'll have very big ears from now on." Enough said. Owen put *Double Oh* in gear and idled out of the fleet on his way to the tuna dealer in Green Harbor.

Chapter 20

Special Gear & Tactics

Any fishery will spawn new gear or at least bring about changes to the tried and true ways of capturing the prey in attempting to improve the catch ratio. This is especially true when the prey is as intelligent, powerful, and adaptable as the bluefin. The power becomes evident when you observe your first hook-up and the intelligence is shown when the fish uses every means available to free itself and by so doing it is able to out smart the best of skippers.

Now we come to the adapting part of the tuna's make up. I'm not talking about adapting to its environment over years of evolution, I'm talking about its ability to adapt quickly to a situation in which it finds itself in harm's way and immediately develops countermeasures to try to escape that situation. This uncanny ability is given credence by many experienced captains who have learned that no two tunas ever act the same and that bluefin always seem to come up with some new method to try to gain their freedom. This adaptability has, in turn, produced some of the most innovative, and yes, imaginative fishermen involved in any fishery. Here are just a few of the gear changes and tactics that have been developed in the last half of the 20th century by these mostly unknown highliners.

A Trip To The Supermarket

In mid-August of 1977 the mate and I had returned from the SW corner of the Bank after a long unsuccessful day of "chop & plop." We fueled up *Misty,* scrubbed her clean, put two boxes of fresh herring in the cooler and iced them down. After consulting with Bruce, I made out a shopping list of items that we were either out of or getting very low on; things that we would need for the next day's fishing.

On the way to the supermarket I stopped at the hardware store and picked up two cans of spray paint; one dark maroon and one flat black. (We used the maroon paint to darken our Sampson cord lines when they began to fade and the flat black to dull anything bright or shiny, including the hooks.)

At the supermarket I received some funny looks from some of the other customers; it isn't often you see someone with a three day beard, dressed in dirty work clothes, wearing knee-high boots and smelling of sweat and day-old chum, pushing a cart around the local A&P.

When I reached the check-out counter, a sweet grandmotherly lady behind me watched as I unloaded my cart onto the conveyer: Two black magic markers, a package of rubber bands, a Bic lighter, two bags of potato chips, a six pack each of Dr. Pepper and Pepsi, a bag of multicolored balloons, a box of Poppycock, cookie cutter, foam cups, a tube of zinc oxide, a bottle of olive oil, and a box of trash bags. The lady smiled and asked who was having a birthday, my son or my daughter? I replied that there was no imminent birthday. "I'm just picking up some things to go tuna fishing tomorrow." On my way to the exit, I overheard her, as she turned to the woman next in line and said: "Well I declare, he ought to go to a tackle store if he wants to buy things to fish with!"

Things on the list and their uses:

Black magic markers - for a quick dry touch-up of terminal tackle.

Rubber bands - used to snub a tuna-bullet until fish is hooked. (see below)

Bic lighter - used to fuse end of Dacron lines.

Balloons - tied to running line as a bobber to control depth of hook-bait.

Olive or Cod Liver Oil - mixed with chum-soup to "sweeten" the chum-slick.

Trash bags - used in place of balloons to catch more wind, when wind and current are weak and balloons will not deploy baits away from hull.

Foam cups - tape, upside down, to top of leader to slow the descent of hook-bait to the same speed of chum chunks. To speed up descent just tear away some of the inverted cup. (See below.)

Cookie cutter - used to chop chum.

Zinc oxide - for ears, nose, neck and cheekbones. The original, and still the best, sun block.

Dr. Pepper, Pepsi, Poppycock, and Potato chips - necessary creature comforts.

Anchor Retrieval System

Once you haul a heavy anchor from a depth of 150 feet or more, you acquire a natural aversion to the task. Once is enough. It is especially distasteful at the end of a long, hot day of tuna fishing. At this point, you'll want to buy a deck-mounted winch, (anywhere from $500 to $1,000 and up.) or put together your own easy and foolproof system (using only four easy components).

I don't know who came up with the idea, but I do know many tuna fishermen, myself included, who would like to buy him a drink in grateful appreciation. It has only four parts, three of which you probably have aboard your boat; a tuna ball (buoy), a large stainless steel snap with a swivel base and a three or four foot length of line that matches your anchor line in diameter. The fourth component is the stainless steel ring you can purchase at most marine supply stores or you can make your own out of 3/8in. stainless bar. (see photo.)

When you are ready to head for the barn, you idle forward so you can lead your anchor line aft, along either gunwale. Slip the ring over the rode, attach the snap line and tuna ball to the ring, and place the system in the water abaft your transom. Now steam off on a course to take you toward where your anchor lies.

The system will allow the anchor line to slide through the ring, and the tension of the water on the ball (plus the lifting power of the ball) will break the anchor loose. As you continue to steam, the anchor will be lifted to the surface until the chain goes through the ring, leaving the anchor hanging by its flukes, three or four feet below the ball.

Now you only need to flake the rode into a fish box as you steer toward the ball. When you reach the ring, pick up the

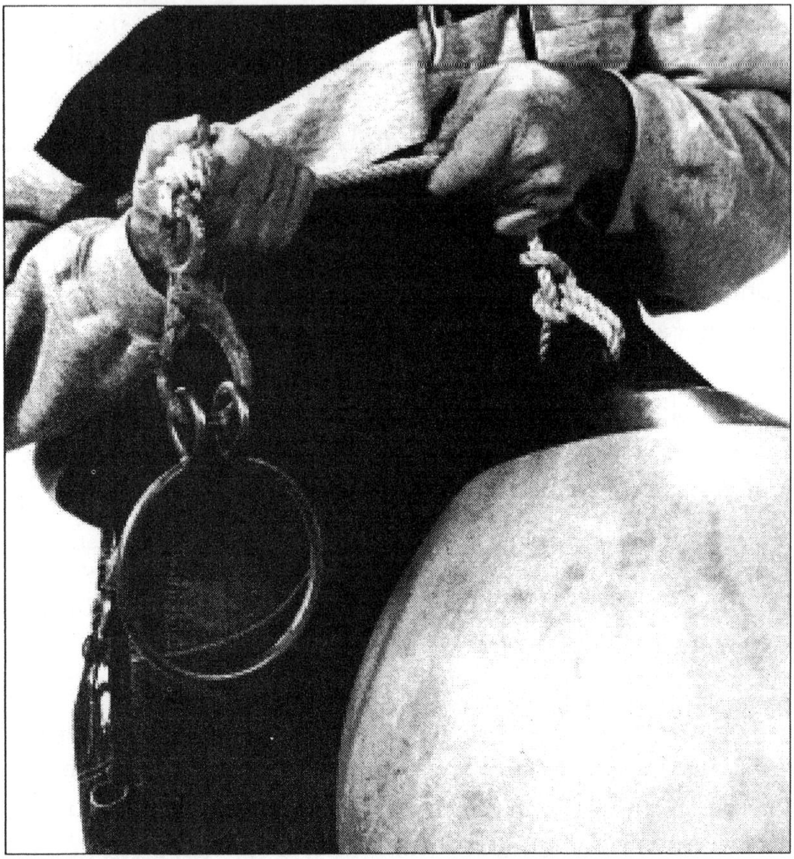

system and anchor, detach the system and place the chain and anchor in the box atop the rode. Your line is now ready for the next time you anchor, and if you plan to be in water of the same depth, you don't even need to unhitch it from your bow-cleat.

Quick Release

Fast action is critical on the hook-up. Being able to drop off your anchor ball quickly can make the difference between catching or losing a fish. I have used a pelican hook, a snap swivel with a spring-loaded plunger, and sometimes even an extra crewmember as quick release devices.

All of these contrivances worked under test conditions; but in real situations, they either failed or slowed our progress, getting underway. Capt. Joe Eldridge gave me the answer: A never-fail release, with no moving parts, made of Sampson cord according to the following description:

> Take a length of line, long enough to reach from the bow-cleat to the bridge, and add eight more feet. Run line through the eye at the end of the anchor line, and form a loop big enough to place over the bow cleat and reach beyond the bow chock. Tie a half hitch in a loop, leaving about six inches to the bitter end. Next, finish off the knot as you would when tying your shoes (no need to double-knot). Place the loop over the bow cleat, with the knot near the cleat, and run the rest of the loop forward with one side in the bow-chock and the other side free. The tuna ball and the end of the anchor line should now be forward of your boat's bow. Secure the standing line to some place easily accessible when a hook-up occurs. A quick tug on the standing line will untie your "shoe" and release the boat. You are now ready to take up the fight.

Harpoons

Webster's dictionary definition: a barbed spear with a line attached to it, used for spearing whales or other large sea animals.

This tells it all, in very simple terms. The harpoon was developed by whalers to make it possible for them to kill and bring to market the planet's most magnificent mammals (humans included). Thank God, we have gained enough wisdom to almost completely eliminate that practice. My Pennsylvania-Dutch mother used to say, "We get too soon old and too late smart."

The modern version of the harpoon evolved from its awkward predecessor into a balanced shaft of tubular aluminum, with a detachable dart that fits on the shank, and is tied to a running line (usually Sampson cord) about 60 feet in length. The running line is connected to some 200 feet of pot warp with a tuna ball on the other end.

Tuna boats with long pulpits will have several throwing-harpoons aboard. They will range in length from 10 to 14 feet, depending on the height of the stand, above the surface.

High-liners customize their sticks to their own specifications so they will have a weapon that is completely comfortable in their hands, and provide them with the most accurate throw.

The cockpit-harpoon is one of the most useful tools developed for the tuna fishery. It is set up in the same way as the throwing-harpoon, but is only six to eight feet in length. It is designed for use in the cockpit to take the place of the flying-gaff.

The flying-gaff has to be one of the most awkward and dangerous pieces of fishing gear ever devised. It is an oversized gaff with a detachable, barbless hook to which you tie about 30' of line. The end of the line is secured to a cleat. When a fish is ready to be taken, you wire the fish alongside the boat and the mate slides the flying-gaff shaft over the victim and then pulls

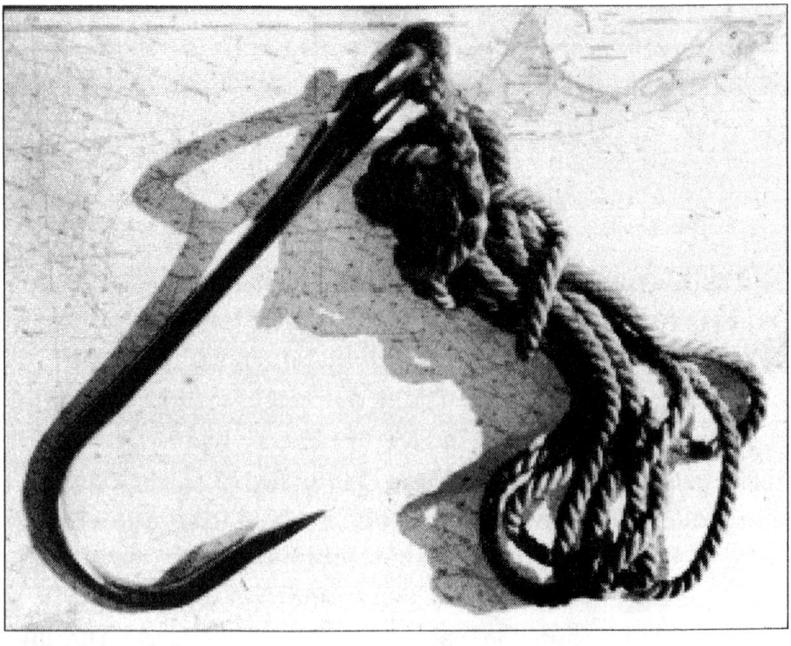

Just lying ther e, the flying gaf f/meat hook looks vicious.

the hook's point back, into the fish.

The mere touch of the shaft on a bluefin's back can cause a violent explosion of activity. I have seen all hell break loose sometimes, before the mate could even sink the hook. I also observed a mate successfully plant a flying gaff in a fish that was still a bit "green" (not ready to be taken). The fish charged off, taking the line, the cleat, and the mate with him. (The mate was rescued immediately, and suffered only a sprained hand from a turn of the line that had wrapped around his wrist when he tried to stop the fish.)

In both of the cases above, the fish were lost. The two reasons for the losses: The angler did not let off on the drag when the tuna was brought to the gaff, so the sudden tightening of the line on the reel snapped the line with the sound of a gunshot. In the case where the mate and gear went overboard, the fault fell on the skipper. He had miscalculated the condition of the quarry and ordered the crew to take a fish that was still too green. (See "Tactics" below).

The cockpit harpoon, on the other hand, is usually set up with about 100' of running line coiled into a milk-crate or similar plastic box with a tuna ball on the bitter end. Once stuck, if the fish takes all of the line and the ball overboard, you just let him go. All you need do then is "follow the bouncing ball" until it stops, and retrieve both ball and fish.

Chum Soup

The preparing of this delicacy is usually left to the newest member of the crew. The experienced seamen always find some way to be "busy" at other, more important tasks, when it's time to prepare the "soup"; and invariably, they'll make sure they are somewhere up-wind of the preparation

The utensils: a five gallon bucket, an old broom handle or other three foot stick, a stainless steel cookie-cutter, (preferably one with a long handle) a heavy-duty ladle, a bait knife, and a cutting board.

The ingredients for an effective chum soup include: one or two quarts of sea water, one quart of cod-liver oil (or for those who need to watch their cholesterol, one quart of virgin olive oil) and 20 to 30 pounds of finely chopped oily fish, such as herring, mackerel or menhaden. (Menhaden is an Algonquin Indian word meaning "fertilizer" — how appropriate.)

Directions: prepare oily fish by cutting or chopping into small chunks. Place in bucket. Add cod-liver oil and seawater. Use the cookie-cutter to mince ingredients to a smooth, fine, loose puree. Use an old broom handle to stir. Remember to stir again, just before broadcasting each ladle-full into the water, behind the transom. (Note: for best results, the use of three or four day-old oily fish is highly recommended. The strong odor insures a seamlessly steady slick, as the assigned broadcaster works to quickly empty the bucket!)

Tuna Bullets

This ingenious device was developed because tuna have teeth. Although their teeth are rather small for an animal of their size, they can easily bite through, and indeed, shred the best monofilament leaders. (We never worried about this problem, in the '70s. We were using 456 lb test 7-stranded cable for our leaders.)

A tuna bullet is made of a two-foot length of stiff tubing, usually automobile brake line, and a lead weight (about 2 lbs), shaped like a football with a hole, the diameter of the tubing, down the center. The weight is split length-wise so it can be attached over one end of the tube and held in place with strong rubber bands.

To create the bullet, slide the tube over the leader, weight first (before attaching the hook to the terminal end). The weight should be near the top of the leader. At the bottom of the tube, pull three or four inches of leader up the outside of the tube and secure the doubled-over leader to the tube with rubber bands. This will hold the bullet at the top of the leader until a strike, or hook-up, straightens the leader, allowing the bullet to slide down and into the tuna's mouth. The tube will reach the hook and act as chaffing gear to protect your leader from the biting, scraping teeth of your prey. The split weight will often break away during the fight.

Zappers

Fishermen come from many disciplines: teachers, doctors, lawyers, state and local policemen, contractors, plumbers, electricians, etc., etc. Many of them bring ideas from their vocation into their fishing and if the ideas work, it is only a matter of time before the rest of the fishing community picks up on them.

The use of zappers must have come from an electrician, or at least someone versed in the use of electricity. It is a device used mainly by harpooners. As soon as a tuna is harpooned, the circuit is closed, sending a high voltage charge to the dart, rendering the fish unconscious (or at least numb), allowing the fisherman to handle the fish right away. The idea is to eliminate the trauma of the struggle-for-freedom, and thus bring to market a better product which will, of course, command a better price

Airplanes

The use of aircraft as spotters for the fishery has been around for many years. First used by the seiners, and then as the value of the fishery rose, they were employed by the boats in the harpoon category, and eventually by many of those in the general category.

As the 20th century drew to a close, the use of spotter aircraft was another factor that was splitting the tuna fishing community. Just one more thing that focuses on access and allocation, instead of thinking about the resource and its availability to all. When it comes to the protection of our marine resources, I'd like to paraphrase my mother's saying in that we get too soon smart, too late wise.

Tactics

There were so many fishermen involved in the tuna fishery, (as the new century began, some 26,000 federal permits had been issued), that it is impossible to list all the tactics used in the attempts to best the bluefin. If a high-liner tells one of his fishing buddies about a method of capture he has found to be valid, it is only a matter of time - a very short time - before that tactic becomes common practice among the sharpies.

Here are some generic tactics used by many of the more successful tuna men. I might lay claim to being the first to use one of them, but then again, others might easily have come up with the same idea, when stymied by a smart and stubborn fish.

The Captain's Basic Responsibilities

When it comes to a rod and reel, with the angler working from a fighting chair, he is basically a power winch! (Yet, I've seen some of these "power-winches" burn out after only a few minutes of cranking.) Over the years, I have observed anglers who range from the very sharp (those who seem to understand the fish and instinctively react to the problems as they become apparent), to the very dull (those that don't even know which way to crank the handle).

It only takes a minute or two of observation before you can place an angler into one of what I like to call the "Clint Eastwood Categories". All anglers fall into one of these three basic groups: "The Good, The Bad and The Ugly."

If an angler is "Good," he listens to the captain and the mate, and carries out their orders quickly and efficiently, and sometimes even seems to anticipate the actions of the prey.

If he is "Bad," he will need lots of encouragement, support, detailed instruction, and sometimes a figurative kick-in-the-ass to get a jump-start on the fight. This category is by far the largest, not because the fishermen are really "bad" per se, but because very few have had the experience of hooking-up and fighting a bluefin. Believe me, it is very easy to become overwhelmed by their sheer power.

As for the "Ugly," he might as well kiss his quarry good-bye. Anglers in this category either think they know it all, or they can't (or won't) take direction. In some cases, the term "slowlearner" might be more applicable than "ugly."

Successful tuna fishing is very much a team effort, and if the angler doesn't contribute to that effort, he becomes "the player who always fumbles the ball."

There are two reasons why the captain is the main person aboard any vessel that catches the fish. First: He makes (or should make) all the decisions regarding the capture of the quarry. Second: He handles all the maneuvers of the vessel, which is the most important piece of "fishing gear" used to bring about a successful end to the struggle. It is used to counter the actions of the fish and apply the proper pressure to tire the fish. It must be maneuvered with agility to place it in the proper attitude to assist the angler and crew with their work, and its port or starboard quarter must be neatly positioned next to the fish when it's ready to be taken.

The ready-to-be-taken determination is the most critical decision for all captains, and they don't always make the right one. I once saw a mate receive a broken arm (from one blow of a tuna's tail) while trying to place a tail-rope on a green fish.

The captain had misjudged the readiness of the fish. It is at this time when most fish are lost, because this crucial decision was made too early in the fight. A good, experienced captain must not allow the crew, or himself to become too anxious. It's a fine line between when the fight is almost over, and really over.

The three most (over-) used excuses for the loss of a fish (spit the hook... broke the leader... snapped the line), in many cases, are really the result of a miscalculation, by the captain.

Of course, if the captain pulls rank, he can blame the mate (for acting too slow), or the angler (for not releasing the drag), or the gaffer (for not being ready), or any other crewmember (for any number of other indiscretions). Ultimately, since he makes all the decisions and handles the vessel, it is the captain who should bear the responsibility. Any fisherman who takes on the privileges afforded to a captain should also assume the responsibilities of that position. The captain is the one person aboard most responsible for the successful capture of Mr. Bluefin.

Each time the determination to take the quarry presented itself, I reminded myself to back off a moment, and think of the famous wine-maker. To paraphrase his ad, I vowed to "take no fish before its time".

During any phase of a fish-fight, from hook-up to tail-rope, it is a good idea to maintain decorum and quiet, so the captain and mate can communicate easily, and so the entire crew can stay "on the same page." (I've seen chaotic crews who weren't even in the same book!)

All successful tuna-catching boats have a quick-thinking, knowledgeable mate. The mate is the chief of the cockpit. He is responsible for the safety and well being of the angler. He must see that the captain's orders are carried out, either by acting alone or with the help of other crewmembers. A mate's most important asset is communication. He must be able to communicate any changes in the attitude of the prey, or the angler, to the captian. Receiving constant up-dates on the status of the fish and the condition of the cockpit enables the captain to make educated decisions at crucial times. The give-and-take between captain and mate often makes the difference between success and failure.

Tactics For The Fight

Space To Work

A man who kept a pet lion in his home, when asked where the lion slept, replied, "Anywhere he wants." If you ask a fisherman where a bluefin swims, the answer is the same.

If you hook-up, while in a fleet of boats, the best thing to do is to just hold on and allow the fish to take you through and away from the fleet. If at all possible, keep track of the direction and position for the fish, so you might be able to "urge" it to change direction by using engine power. Whatever you do, do it gently at this stage of the game. Until your prey is clear of the fleet, try not to stir him up. Once clear, you can put-the-boots-to-it. (See Chapter 13)

Most of the other boats in the fleet will drop off their anchor balls and get out of the way if your fish comes in their direction. "Walking" a fish out of the fleet is somewhat like walking a dog down a crowded street ... except that the watery leash is a hell of a lot longer.

Towing

One thing to remember is the fact that the bluefin is a powerful opponent, and his most outstanding characteristic is stamina. That stamina must be overcome, if you expect to bring one home.

The name of the game is to tire your opponent, and the most common method is to let the fish tow the boat. This is a good idea, if you use it as an opportunity to settle into the fight, and let the crew settle into their assigned duties.

The danger in the tow-the-boat tactic is that it is often allowed to carry on for too long. You must never let the fish rest. Once he overcomes the inertia, a fish can easily tow a boat at upwards of two to three knots. Once in this groove, he can get his second wind, and the fight falls essentially into neutral, with neither opponent holding the upper hand.

In the towing mode, the fish is usually near the surface because a straight pull is easier than one with a downward angle. It is a good idea to have the angler haul back on the rod periodically, to let the prey know you mean business, and that you want his butt. "Jabbing" the fish, thus, will often turn a "Mexican stand-off" into an advantage for the boat. By provoking the fish to swim deeper, you make his work of towing the boat much harder. The angler, now, has only to ride-the-bucket-harness, or just hang-on.

Paralleling - Mirroring

From the instant of the hook-up, the captain must become aggressive. He should be thinking only of ways to keep that fish working hard. Agitate, agitate, agitate! As mentioned above, don't ever allow a bluefin to get his second wind.

Once you have plenty of room for the fight, one of the best

ways to tire your opponent is to maneuver the boat to a position, parallel with the fish, matching its speed and heading. The drag on a hundred yards of bowed line being pulled through water, at a 90° angle to your course, is the same as towing a 4' X 8' sheet of plywood, flat, against the current - a very effective tool for eroding your fish's stamina!

If the fish changes speed or direction, the captain simply mirrors its actions with the boat. If the fish slows its pace, it is time for the angler to jab it back into action.

Charging the Boat

This is one subject the captain should address long before the boat even arrives at the fishing grounds. This is a real "what-if" that demands instant reaction by the entire crew. Being forewarned can make all the difference in the outcome of this scenario.

When a fish charges a boat, the chances of it gaining freedom are better than at any other time. Regardless of the species being sought, or the method and tackle being used, all fishermen should know that slack lines are a No-No! A slack line can give the fish a chance to spit the hook, or fray the line on rough objects, or, with a sudden burst of speed, snap the line or leader.

I was always very specific about the crew's assignments, should a fish turn on the boat. It was my job to determine a new direction, roughly perpendicular to the fish, and to increase speed enough to create a bow in the line (so it would soften the shock of the line as it became tight again). The mate must first loosen the drag by about half, and then make sure the angler and the rod are always facing the point where the line enters the water. The angler must crank as fast as possible, for as long as it takes, to again come up tight to the fish.

Instructions to the rest of the crew usually consisted of, "Get the hell out of the cockpit, and shut-up!"

Is Our Adversary Tiring, Yet?

At the mid-point in any fight, many captains begin to feel a dilemma. They start to wonder who has the reserve strength to carry the fight to a final victory - the fish, or the angler?

The smart thing to do is to put some pressure on the angler. As Captain Don Hebert always said, when asked what was the most important thing to remember when trying to out-smart a giant tuna, "Never give 'em a Goddamn inch!"

Here, again, the word "agitate" takes center stage; and here is where a good mate can make a big difference in the battle of wits and wills. The mate can use a variety of methods to encourage, cajole, and – if necessary – threaten the angler to keep working. He can keep the angler "refreshed" by pouring cooling water over his head, offering a drink of cold beer, even dumping ice down his back as an effective shock treatment. The mate or captain must do anything possible to tip the balance of power in the angler's favor. They must do whatever it takes to make the angler work at gaining line.

"Lift and Crank!" But, remember, there is no need to hurry. Just work steadily to shorten the distance between you and the fish.

This is one time when humans have an advantage over the bluefin. When a fish shows more fight, increase the pressure on it. Have the angler hike himself above the seat, by cranking in the line, and then lean back and lower himself, using his weight to pull the fish closer to the boat. This use of kinetic energy imparted to the rod lets the fish know he is loosing the tug-of-war.

If all this fails, and the angler burns out, we still have one last-ditch chance of winning the battle; we can simply substitute a fresh fighter to finish the job. The fish doesn't have that option.

A Bluefin's Last-Ditch Tactic

Tuna have a propensity for improvising new ways to escape capture. Each individual seems to have the capacity to innovate. If the captain is successful in countering each new surprise move, the odds of winning the battle are in his favor.

However, there is one tactic that seems to be common to

almost all giants. When they realize their opponent can't be out smarted, and the range to their antagonist is only 20 or 30 yards and closing, they try to reach the protection of the bottom.

The drag on the reel should be tightened to the point where the fish cannot pull any line from the spool. The result is that the prey can only swim in a tight circle, perhaps 50 to 100 feet straight down.

If the captain and mate do not already know on which side of the mouth the fish is hooked, now is the time to make this determination. Circling clockwise means the hook is on the right side of the jaw and the fish should be taken on the port quarter of the vessel.

Slowly maneuver the boat to place the rod tip to port and just a little ahead of the beam. The line will be describing a cone-shape in the water with the fish swimming under the boat and aft, then completing the cone-shape away from the boat and forward.

The angler must now try to winch the fish up to within the range of the cockpit harpoon. The captain can help by putting the boat in gear, at idle, with the helm hard over to port and circle counter-clockwise. (The reason for taking the fish on the port side is so it will circle under the boat from forward to aft and thus reappear near the port corner of the transom, where the harpoon-man will have the best view of a clean shot.)

Patience is the word here. The closer the bluefin can be winched toward the surface, the better the shot. Usually, the mate handles the harpoon and, of course, it is his decision as to when to take his best shot, depending on how many times the fish was allowed to circle, and how near the surface the angler was able to winch Mr. Bluefin.

If the fish is hooked on the left side, he will circle counter clockwise, and therefore all of the above procedures will need to be reversed, with the fish being taken on the starboard quarter.

Planing the Fish

Often, a fish will "set its feet", and refuse to be reeled that last

30 or 40 feet to bring it within cockpit-harpoon range. If this happens, the concern becomes just how much pressure the tackle can take before exceeding its breaking strength, and/or will the excess pressure pull the hook. As long as the fish is able to stay straight down while circling, and prevent the angler from winching him any closer, he can maintain another "Mexican stand-off".

If the tackle is deemed to be near its limit, the next decision is actually a no-brainer for the captain. Let's say the fish is hooked on the right side, and is circling clockwise some 40 feet below the port side. The vessel is in idle, making a slow turn to port. All the captain has to do is bring the helm to amidships and assume a straight-ahead course. The cone-shape being scribed by the line that is straight down will gradually rise. The cone will then be aft of the transom and the fish will still be circling clockwise – in an almost horizontal attitude, aft of the vessel - to the right and downward, then to the left and upward. Once the prey is in this position, the angler should be able to slowly gain line; especially when the fish is on the near-surface half of the cone.

As the fish is drawn within sticking range, the captain should put the helm hard to port, and the mate should be at the ready with the cockpit-harpoon, when the fish is at the top of the cone and abeam to port.

Chumming

Chumming has one thing in common with filleting – I have never found two fishermen who agree on the best way to do either task! There is really no definitive method. The object, of course, is to entice tuna to your "lunch counter" and then be served a snack with a hook in it.

The first thing to do is to let the fish know the diner is open for business, and that your menu is the best in the fleet. The best tuna men do agree on one point: chum made from the oiliest ingredients, and the use of live "entrees" (the bait with the hook) is the best way to bring customers to your lunch counter. At this point, all agreement ends.

How do you draw the "customers" to your particular lunch counter, when there are so many available? How do you get the fish to eat the entrees? How do you serve the meal in the most enticing way?

To answer the first question: you have to get their attention, by creating a slicker slick than the other nearby chummers. The sharpies will always start their slicks by using excessive amounts of chunks, enhanced by plenty of chum-soup. (This ploy is the same as that used by the burger-joints that throw sliced onion on the grille and let the hunger-inducing odor waft out to the street.)

There are two rules of thumb to which you should always adhere: #1 – The hook-baits should be the same size as the chum chunks, and # 2 – the hook- bait must always be kept in the chum slick.

Fly-Rodders always say you have to "match the hatch." When you chop and plop, you are actually creating your own hatch; so it makes sense to have the hook-bait match the size of the chunks in your hatch.

Scenario #1

Chunks of chum will sink at a given rate. If there is no current, they will go straight down. This makes it easy; all you need to do is throw the chum at the balloons holding the hook bait, and the slick will form from the surface down. You know the chum is doing its job. The bad news: any no-current situation will usually last only a few minutes during each tide.

Scenario #2

If the chum is sinking at a rate of 10 feet for every 10 feet of distance it is swept aft by the current, it is descending at a 45° angle. To make sure you have a hook-bait in the slick, with this strength of current, it should be hanging 20 feet below the balloon, with the balloon 20 feet aft of the transom. Your hook-bait will be in the slick only if you are broadcasting the chum from the stern. Broadcasting the chum from amidships will mean the slick will most likely pass below the hook-bait.

Of course, all other baits should be deployed at the proper depth and distance, keeping the 45° angle in mind.

In each of those two scenarios, chumming is easy to figure; but since the speed of the current is ever-changing, effective chumming can become a mathematical nightmare! Under extreme moon tides, it can become necessary to throw the chum forward of the bow, just to get it down to five feet as it passes the stern. Between the fast moving current of the moon tide and the stillness of slack water, there are a multitude of conditions that change the effectiveness of chumming. (Einstein may have figured out the Theory of Relativity, but I bet he'd be challenged as a chummer.)

The most successful chum fishermen are constantly checking, adjusting, and repositioning their hook-baits in response to the changing tidal conditions in an effort to keep their hook-bait in the chum slick.

Here are some other special tactics developed by some of the most successful tuna takers.

Most Important Tidbit

If you are bringing a fish to market, you obviously want the best price offered. Take the time to learn how best to bleed the fish, ice it down and wrap in a Mylar-blanket. *(See below)* Remember, fish flesh is very sensitive to heat, and it will loose its color, firmness, and taste rapidly, if allowed to become warmer than the water it was taken from. To get the best price you should bring in the best product.

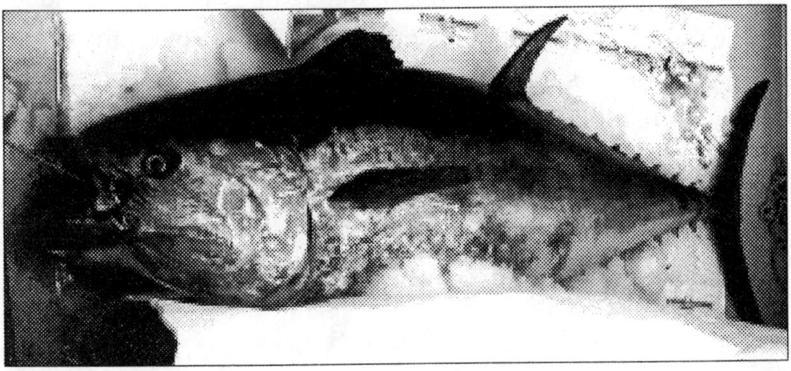

Enhance Your Darts

Darts are designed to toggle when the line comes tight, as the fish reacts to being stuck. If they do not toggle, the dart will pull out. (The fish now has a fresh wound and is angry as hell.) To improve the chances of your dart penetrating, and toggling properly, you must first sharpen the two edges to a razor-blade condition, using a fine file. Next, place each tail fin in a vice and bend it up to a 45° angle. (See below) This will insure the dart will toggle - provided the harpoon is thrown with enough force to penetrate the tuff hide!

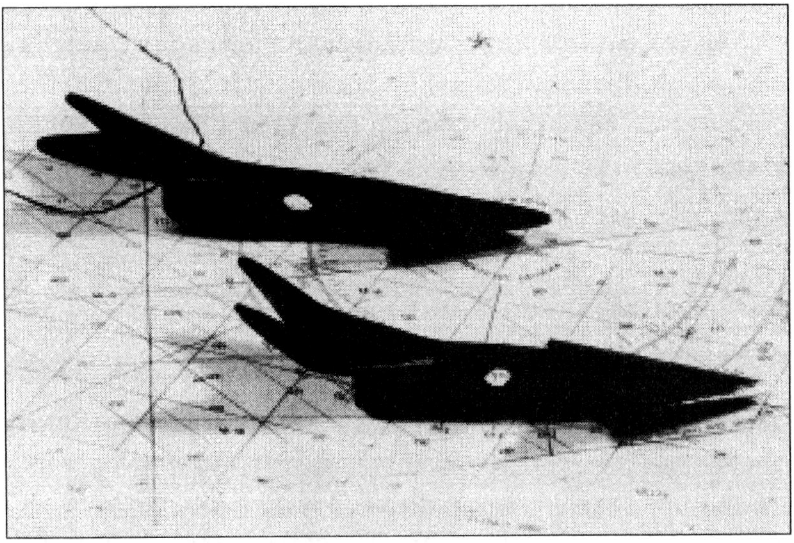

Water Spray

Attach your wash-down hose to the tip of an outrigger and deploy. When you have the fish near the boat, turn on the wash down pressure. As the spray hits the surface, it will create the sound of a school of bait-fish trying to escape preditors. (See Chapter 14.)

Tuna are as curious as cats and they just have to check out the sound of baitfish in a frenzy. This will work best if you have a live bluefish or mackerel to liveline under the spray.

Foam Cups

There are times when bluefin are feeding in your chum slick, so close to the stern, that the term "hand feeding" is applicable. I have often watched a fish swim up the slick, eating every bite of chum (except the ones with the hooks, of course). The hooked chunks are tethered, and therefore do not have the same motion in the current as the free chunks. Also, the weight of the hook makes them sink faster. This difference in speed and motion is noticed by the intelligent bluefin and they have learned to avoid the loaded chunks.

How do you make the hooked baits match the pace of loose chum chunks? Attach a foam cup, lip down, to the leader at 4 to 5 feet above the hook-bait. The cup acts as a water bourn parachute. If the cup makes the hook-bait descend too slowly, tear away some of the cup, until its decent matches that of the unarmed chunk.

Reverse Pulpit

What do you do when the fish are swimming up your slick, eating every bit of your chum, but ignoring the hook-baits? To add insult to injury, they even seem to be following you, but break off their pursuit just short of coming within harpoon range, off your transom.

Captain Don Hebert (Chapter 14) had the answer. He rigged a pulpit on the aft end of the White Lady's bridge deck, so the stand placed him about 15 feet abaft its transom. This made White Lady the first and only double-ended stick boat. It looked very strange anchored in the midst of the chum fleet - but what the hell, it worked.

Trash Bags

When wind and current are so weak that there isn't even enough force to even blow a balloon away from the hull, your hook-bait will often refuse to deploy behind the transom. Under these conditions, your baits will hang around the hull and do nothing but aggravate the captain and crew. With the baits hanging next to the hull, a hook-up could potentially cause problems with tangled lines, including your anchor line, or result in a break-off if the fish pulls the line across the hull's bottom.

By using a blown-up trash bag in place of the balloons, you will create a bigger target for what little wind there might be, to blow the baited lines clear of the hull. It might help create a feeling that if you do hook-up, you'll be able to at least clear the rest of the lines.

Tail-Wrapped

This is not a tactic that any tuna-tangler can deliberately employ. It's more of a "situation" that a tuna finds himself in, rather than something the fisherman instigates. In fact, it is something that, once in a while, just happens.

In its struggle to gain freedom, the fish will sometimes get a turn of the leader around its tailfin.

When this happens, the angler will feel, and see, a vibration at the tip of the rod. Tail wrapping can occur at any time during the fight. I have found that a tail-wrap often occurs while the fish is in the boat-towing mode.

The leader can partially restrict one of the gill plates and, as a result, the fish cannot "breath" efficiently. (I once hooked a crazy fish that was somehow able to roll enough to cause the leader to close both his gill plates. He expired in short order, and when we brought him to the surface, we found the leader had also wrapped around both caudal pentacles.)

When a fish gets tail-wrapped, the best thing to do is to do nothing. The decreased capacity of the gill to supply oxygen to the blood should tire the fish faster, rendering him ready-to-take, that much sooner.

Condoms

Condoms are used in many creative ways, these days. Even the original purpose for which they were designed has changed. Now, instead of being simply for preventing pregnancy, they are touted as a device to insure safe sex. They are also the best product to keep dirt out of a freshly bandaged cut, and to keep the bandages dry, while showering or working around water. And what, do you suppose, is the second most popular use of condoms, on college campuses? They make great water balloons!

The use of condoms in place of colorful balloons to suspend hook-baits is not exactly common practice; you might say they are sometimes prone to "indecent exposure" when in public view during the tuna season. Once recognized, it's evident that they are not being employed in the manner for which they were intended (for that matter, neither are the colorful balloons).

I have to admit that, bobbing on the surface (standing straight up, like a three-foot phallic symbol) they do present a fair amount of entertainment value. Still, I fail to see the advantage they might bring to the tuna fishery. Form follows function, yes? But this function has nothing to do with that form!

Pro's and Con's of condom use as a fishing tool.

_Pro - stronger, longer, and taller than balloons

_ Con - not as colorful as balloons

_Pro - has additional uses when fishing ends

_ Con - can be expensive with many hook-ups

_Pro - good for the attention-seeker

_ Con - bad for those with sexual hang-ups

I have no particular objection to the use of condoms as fishing floats. After all, they do work, and I suppose they look better than the blown-up latex gloves I once saw being used by a surgeon/fisherman. Latex is stronger than rubber, but, really, who can be serious about fishing with a bunch of inverted udders bobbing behind your transom?!

Chapter 21

Observations And Snippets

The following paragraphs are actual incidents and observations that I had the privilege and pleasure of watching while fishing for bluefin over the last 35. In most of these snippets, I have used real names because I feel no need to protect the innocent or the guilty when reporting real happenings.

Whirly Birds & The Moon At High Noon

As the country moved into the 1980s, we noticed that there seemed to be heightened surveillance of the tuna fleet by helicopters. They were reacting to reports of boats transferring tuna to other boats that had not hooked up. (The deal was the receiving boat would sell the fish and then pay half of the receipts to the catcher boat.) *White Lady* was on their list of suspects. One day a CG whirly bird was circling *White Lady*, taking photographs, while flying very low and so close to her that chances of a hook-up were imposable. Capt. Don was pissed off, and rightly so, but his son Gary had the solution: He climbed the mast to the crows nest and dropped his pants!

Somewhere in the CG archives there is a picture of Don's mate mooning the whirly bird as it flew away to check the next boat on the list!

The Three Ball Tuna

Some tuna display their speed by emptying a tuna basket and pulling the tuna ball overboard, before the fisherman can grab the line in an attempt to slow the adversary. In many cases the fisherman didn't even get a chance to snap a safety line to the ball end of the line with the screaming fish hooked to it. When this happens, the skipper merely has to follow the ball until it stops moving, pick it up and haul in the fish. Several times I had a ball go overboard and immediately disappear below the surface. The speed had been joined by the raw strength of my enemy.

Taking a ball under water, even for a short time, usually breaks the will of the fish and results in an easy capture. There is always an exception to the normal flow of events.

White Lady hooked-up and before Don could even pull the quick release, the ball was overboard and under water. I noticed a safety line peeling over the transom with Don trying to "get-a-grip" to stop the fish. The second ball flew out of the cockpit, peeled water for several feet and disappeared under the surface. The mate had snapped a second safety line to the first one and Don calmly picked up its ball and tossed it over board just as the end of the line left the basket.

He spun *White Lady* around and started following the third ball as it headed westward kicking up considerable spray. As he passed Misty, he shrugged his shoulders and exclaimed: "I've never had a fish take two balls under and still be able to tow a second safety line." With this he gave the finger in the direction of the "hookie" and said: "You're a tough bastard, but I'm gonna getcha, even if you do have a three football field head start!" What amazing speed, strength and stamina. Don told me later, in Green Harbor, that the fish was a 680 pound teenager!

The Success Syndrome

I sometimes think fishermen are more superstitious than those in any other discipline. All it takes to make a fisherman an absolute superstitious nut-cake is to land a fish! It doesn't make any difference if it is caught by skill or just plain luck. Some common results: be sure to wear the same socks every trip, always leave the harbor at the same time, don't change any of the crew members, decide to not shave until you get another tuna, and of course you have to have the same lunch each trip. These superstition acts apply to many other disciplines, including the sports world.

The strange acts that set the fishermen apart? One friend of mine told everyone he was not at all superstitious. This was accepted until we found out he worried that he would forget to tell some other tuna man that he was not superstitious. Another buddy from Green Harbor always urinated over the side before he put any hook baits into the water. He went 15 days with no luck and then had a streak of three fish in three days. I asked him what he did to change his luck? His reply - "I now piss over the transom."

The one that turned out to be the most odorous was the young fisherman who decided he would not bathe until he caught his next tuna, then went over six weeks without even a hook-up!

The Divorce Rate & Booze

Anybody who enters a bar frequented by tuna fishermen is bound to notice that a large percentage of the clientele have had a few too many. In my opinion, this is a result of the very low percentage of successful tuna fisherman. When you go after bluefin day after day and don't even hook a fish it tends to get too you. (See - 31 Days Straight - below.) The high market value and easy entry into the fishery draws many people who have no experience, no skill and no know-how for the fishery. (Statistics indicate, of the 23,000 permits issued, at least 20,000 permit holders will only smell the day-old chum.) Once you have a tiger by the tail, with each succeeding day, it becomes harder to let go: the result is to hide away from your frustrations in a bottle of booze - until you have to try again the next morning. The next steps: Debts, loss of job, paranoid symptoms, and failing friendships. Worse yet: I know five guys who lost their boats, trucks and ultimately their house and property in divorce court!

31 Days Straight

Bruce Hebert (my most tuna-savvy mate) and I agreed to cancel all August charters, the following season, and devote ourselves completely to tuna fishing. Not having to entertain customers, we could leave the harbor early enough to insure a top spot on the SW corner and, with a little luck, could easily double our August income. The going price of bluefin had risen to $12 a pound.

At the end of the first week — no hook-ups. The second week: still no luck and *Misty* was considered to be snake-bit. As the days went on Bruce and I had no reason to speak; our days were on automatic and a blue funk hung over our lives.

31 August - Still no fish and we looked at each other, through bloodshot eyes, trying to figure out which one of us was the Jonah.

At that time the cost for a day of tuna fishing was over $100. (Bait, fuel, tackle and food.) I had given up $4,000 in charters and had put over $3,000 into those thirty-one unproductive tuna trips. Mortgage payments on *Misty* were delinquent. I was looking at losing my boat and my business. On top of all that, Bruce, who was used to making at least $100 a trip, had not made a cent.

The reason I remained in business and still have Bruce as a real friend? Starting on 1 September we broke the drought and brought in a fish each day for seven days straight. The average weight of each of the seven fish was 750 lbs and at $14 per pound — you do the math . . .

The Five-Gallon Bucket

This is the most common fishing put-on. Two things must be present to carry it out: The boat must be trolling for tuna and the victim asleep. Start by hauling in the trolling gear and replace it with, and deploy, a five-gallon bucket. Place boat in gear at idle. Wake the victim/angler by shouting: "We have a hook-up." Place angler in fighting chair and place rod in gimbal. When angler begins taking in line, add some throttle to make line deploy.

Add drama by changing to a new course so the view from the chair looks as if the fish is changing direction. When angler is near exhaustion, return to idle so he can again begin to win the fight. Have crew encourage and praise angler until he sees the bucket. At that instant the fight is over and, so too, maybe some friendships!

One Box Of Chum = Three Fish

Sometimes the fishing gets fabulous. *Misty* had a combo-charter aboard and we were starting the trip by going for tuna. I had one box of chum and just after anchoring on the SW corner, a buddy called and said the bait dealer had run out and asked if I had some to spare. I told him to come alongside and he could have half of mine. Several boats had already hooked-up. After my buddy picked up my chum he picked up one of their anchor balls and started chumming heavily. Ten minutes went by and he hooked-up. One hour later he called on the VHF and said he had tail roped his fish and was headed for the Barn.

Misty was unable to answer the call because we hooked-up just as I picked up the microphone. After tail roping and bleeding our fish, I received another VHF call; this time from *Chanty*. (Stormy Mayo's father was the skipper and Stormy the mate.) "Hey Cap, I heard you have your fish — congratulations. I'm on my way to the corner. Do you have any chum left?" I looked up and saw *Chanty* about three miles dead ahead. "Cap, I'm on my way to Race Point and we're headed right at you. I got a half box for you." He came alongside and we transferred the chum. He wanted to pay for the chum; I told him no way, it had already hooked two fish and I wished him good luck.

Race Point was alive with bluefish. The Charter had a ball belting the big blues to finish off the trip.

Misty was getting underway for Green Harbor when I again spotted *Chanty* passing the RP Buoy. I grabbed my binoculars: Riding on the leading side of the first wake was a giant tuna being towed headfirst. Three for one is pretty good odds!

Stormy Sticks A Green One

I first knew Stormy Mayo as a fifteen year old kid, the mate on his father's charter boat, *Chanty*. (Stormy is now a leading marine biologist for the Center For Coastal Studies, headquartered in Provincetown, Mass.) At that early age he had already developed a passion for the sea and a curiosity about its inhabitants. This incident is just a snippet from an early confrontation with a tuna.

Chanty was lazily returning from an unsuccessful trip to Stellwagen Bank. Stormy was resting on the foredeck when he heard a slight swishing sound just off the starboard side. Swimming along side, just fast enough to pass *Chanty*, was an 800lb. tuna. It moved two or three boat lengths ahead, turned 180° and proceeded aft of *Chanty*.

Stormy quickly rigged the harpoon, carried it to the cockpit and watched as the fish did another 180° turn. When it again reached the transom, Stormy cocked the harpoon and as his father said, "Never harpoon a green fish." Stormy struck. There was no sudden explosive splash. This victim moved off about 30' and then became dormant. After the tail roping, Stormy found the reason why the fish hadn't ripped the harpoon line out of the boat. An earlier fight it had won, over a rod & reel boat, must have completely exhausted it. Trailing from the hook imbedded in its jaw, was a leader, barrel swivel and a bimini-twist double line!

Wacky Behavior - No Bite

Tuna decide when to eat and when not to eat. It seems the decision not to eat is more prevalent on those hot, humid, still and quiet days. Those days also have a profound effect on the fishermen. After several hours of chumming with no hook-ups the boats in the fleet cease serious chumming and it seems the crews become wackos. Here are strange events and procedures observed on some of these dog days.

- The VHF radio becomes flooded with taunting barbs, foul language and obscene jokes. — all aimed at any and all boats on the common channel.
- Crews share their chum with near-by boats. This action soon becomes a test of skill to see how much chum can be splattered

on the crew of the other boat. The game spreads throughout the fleet when its formal name is shouted - Chum fight, chum fight.

• As the chum fights escalate the ammunition from some boats becomes harder and heavier. This makes for more range and accuracy but when the receiving-boat is hit with lead sinkers the chum fight becomes a dangerous and hateful frenzy.

• I watched one boat steam across another boat's bow just ahead of its anchor ball, turn 90° and pull away. Very shortly the anchor ball began following the "steamer" toward the deeper water, with the anchored boat in tow. I later found out that the steaming boat was using a grappling hook, made out of cheap rebar, to un-anchor the victim

• A reaction from one boat can take over the entire fleet when the bite is nil. Many members of the fleet are immediately seen as being woefully unequipped for a hook-up. These boats obviously "have no clue" about how to handle a bluefin if they somehow luck out. All it takes is one boat to evoke the common "label" for these craft and the rest of the fleet will join in. A husky, frog-like croak could be heard, spreading from the source outward in all directions to the far ends of the fleet, "Dink-boat, Dink-boat, Dink-boat..."

• When a day is hot & dry, a cold beer can be a blessing. A couple of six packs can be a detriment. You are sure alcohol has been imbibed to excess when a crewmember from a near-by boat keys his mike and the airwaves are flooded with "Do It To Me One More Time" by The Captain & Tennile. That really wasn't a bad intrusion, until the guy with the mike made it a trio by adding his own slurred, out of sync and out of tune voice.

• The opposite reaction to the chum fights, VHF antics, boozing and "Krappy Karaoke" is shared by those who succumb to the heat: Quit chumming and wind up spread all over the boat in various positions of repose. One skipper always carried a fold-up beach chair, which he placed on the foredeck, reclined on and eventually snoozed in. From a casual observers viewpoint, those crewmembers appeared to be in a comatose state, waiting for the heat and humidity to let up.

Half A Ton and A $20 Bill

Kenny Hebert was often on the Brant Rock town pier as *Misty* was readying to head out to the tuna grounds. He was about 12 years old and was always riding his bicycle. As we departed, he would always say that we would get a thousand-pounder. My mate Bruce would answer with: "Go back home where you belong, little brother."

Kenny Hebert won $20 with his 1,000 pound prediction of the weight of this bluefin.

On 2 September 1978, Bruce and I hooked into a heavy fish that Bruce stuck with the cockpit harpoon after a struggle of 45 minutes. After bleeding, while I was preparing the fish for towing head first, Bruce measured the length and girth and applied the formula for estimating the weight. (W = LG^2 divided by 800) The answer was a fish of about 950 lbs.

We pulled up to the fuel dock and there was Kenny sitting on his ever-present bicycle. He took a look at the tuna and said: "I told you you'd get a thousand-pounder some day." I said it weighed about 950 lbs. Kenny replied: "I got twenty bucks that says it weighs 1,000." "You're on, Kenny," was my rejoinder.

At the weigh-in the weigh master placed discs equal to nine hundred fifty lbs, and then pushed the slide that adds a pound at a time, toward the 50-pound mark. The scale balanced when the slide reached the end, and he announced: "Exactly 1,000 lbs."

I turned to a grinning Kenny, pulled a twenty from my pocket, and handed it to him. He stuffed it into his jeans, jumped on his bike and sped away with all that needed to be said: "I told you so!"

Fighting Chair Placement

The fighting chair is a marvelous piece of fishing gear. It does what it is designed to do so well that the basic form has not been changed since Ernest Hemmingway used one to land huge marlin, near Key West. It is too bad that it is often set up in a bad position so its potential to aid in a tuna fight is nullified.

First, the cockpit must be large enough for the chair to turn at least 300°. From dead astern, 150° to both port and starboard.

Next, with the footrest completely extended, it should clear the interior of the transom, with enough room for a mate to move easily back and forth, when the chair is facing dead aft.

If those two observations are followed you will be placing the chair in an optimum position in your boat's cockpit.

It goes without saying that the chair must be securely anchored to the deck. I always recommend a medal backing plate be mounted under the deck and through bolted to the chair

NOT the best placement for a fighting chair!

flange. One of my friends had a chair come loose while fighting a fish; he was pulled to the transom with the chair in tow and had to finish the fight standing up. The fish was a little over 700 lbs. This was 1978, long before stand-up gear was developed.

Small Boat Advantage

What kind of vessel would make the perfect tuna boat? Over the years I have caught giants, (using rod & reel, handline, and harpoon) from a 21' center console up to a 31' JC. I've seen fish taken by handline from anchored draggers and I've watched the big tuna seiners haul in hundreds of fish by net. All of these vessels catch fish, but each has a drawback.

Most of them are too big and heavy, making it necessary to pull the fish to the boat. It is easier to pull the boat to the fish. Lets zero in on the smaller lighter vessels. What other attributes do these small boats posses?

The big sport-fishermen have the fighting chair mounted in

the stern, which means the boat must be backing down for most of the fight. Speed and maneuverability are nullified. A small light vessel should mount the chair or fighting post in the bow area; this allows the boat to be steered toward the fish and gives it the capability of using its speed to run down the fish when it is stripping line from the spool.

The ability to reel the boat to the fish and then use the forward motion to keep the bow right over the fish makes for a fast efficient fight.

Rod & Reel vs. Handline

During the 1970s and 1980s, whenever a few tuna fishermen got together and began discussing their passions and frustrations with the state of the fishery, one argument would almost always surface. A debate over the best way to tuna fish - Rod & reel vs. handline.

Mankind first learned to harvest from the sea by using a sharpened stick to spear fish for their sustenance — the first harpoon. When man developed a way to make a line, long and strong enough to catch fish, he was able to feed a whole community — the first handline. The next step was to wind the handline on a wooden spool and mount it on a willow branch — the first rod and reel.

Today we know the handline concept is basically the same as originally designed, while the rod & reel concept is constantly evolving. What does each of these concepts offer to the fisherman?

Rod & Reel

Tuna rods now have bent butts that give a mechanical advantage to the angler. This makes it easier to put a bow in the rod, and load it with kinetic energy, to increase the pressure on the fish. The six or seven guides on a tuna rod spread and defuse the stress on the line and the rollers on the guides reduce line friction virtually to zero.

Modern reels have two spool ratios: High speed to gain line quickly when the fish turns toward the boat and a low speed to gain line against a grind-it-out battle with a stubborn fish.

The fighting chair's swivel action allows the angler to always face the fish and the footrest allows him to increase the bow in the rod to exert maximum pressure on the fish.

During the fight, we give the angler anything he needs: feed him, give him beverages, cool him with water over his head, etc. However, you must never give the angler a cigarette. According to the Surgeon Admiral, smoking near a tight tuna line, with a good bow in the rod, can instantaneously cause bleeding from the nose, a possible concussion and the loss of a fish!

Handline

The handline has none of the amenities of the rod, reel and fighting chair mentioned above. It has one advantage over rod & reel — its line strength is much higher. However, that is negated by the fact that the leader strength is usually the same for each method. If you jack up the going leader strength, your chance of hooking-up is nil — just another example of how the tuna's smarts affects the fisherman.

The drag system consists of how much pressure you can apply to the running line with your grip. If the palms get over-heated the "drag system" can be cooled by leaning over the side and plunging the hands into the water. The fisherman can apply only one other advantage. He can double his strength by bending the line over the gun'ell.

Handlining is basically a tug-of-war with the raw power and stamina of the fish - faster, heavier, stronger - fighting for its life on one end and man on the other.

The rise of the handline method roughly paralleled the development of the Japanese market for bluefin tuna.

The Hot Ball

There are times when a boat is anchored in exactly the right spot. Fish seem to be under the boat just waiting for their turn to eat. *Jazz* was at anchor less than 100' feet from *Shitluck*. (That name was real.) At first *Luck* was having trouble boating a fish, and lost her first two hook-ups. Each time, another boat had jumped on her anchor ball and went off with a fish before *Luck* returned for another try. On the third, try she caught her fish, while another boat grabbed her ball and hooked-up.

At this time, the ball had produced six fish; four taken and two dropped. *Luck* was about to haul anchor when a fifth boat offered to haul *Luck's* anchor, if it could use the ball. Permission granted.

My mate said if this boat goes off, maybe we should grab the ball. My reply was that we were only 100' away and there was no reason to move— "Our time will come." Wrong idea!

The mate and I kept a tally: By the time we had used all our chum and hauled our anchor, the hot ball had scored eleven hook-ups with nine different boats, and as far as we knew, nine fish had been taken.

Yellow Boat Yelling

I hate yellow boats. I don't wish to offend all those who prefer boats with that watered down mustard look, but I have two valid reasons for my dislike.

One took place on a day when the bluefish were feeding on the surface with hundreds of birds circling overhead. Misty slowed down and drifted toward the commotion. In short order eight or ten boats had formed a circle with their bows pointed toward the center. All the anglers on the circle of boats were having a great time getting hook-ups on almost every cast. Catching blues on light tackle can be one of fishing's greatest thrills! (These blues were all in the twenty-pound size.)

The sound of a high-powered boat broke the spell. I saw a bright yellow boat streaking for the center of the circle. It stopped in the center and the Capt. looked around wondering, "What is going on?" I yelled back: "Nothing, NOW." The fish were down and the birds had dispersed.

The other reason for my aversion to yellow boats took place while handlining for tuna on Stellwagen Bank, anchored next to a big yellow sport fisherman from Florida. Bruce and I were hoping for a quick hook-up to get away from the pontificating, coming from two of the yellow-yahoo's crew.

Thankfully, I heard Bruce quietly say we were on, as he set the hook. I was clearing the other lines, when the two yahoos started screaming they were hooked-up and issuing orders to the rest of their crew at a volume that could be heard by half of the fleet. In the next instant they were yelling that they had a double hook-up.

Our fish was towing *Misty* stern first, and the "*Yellow-Yahoo*" (as I nicknamed it) seemed to be closing on us stern to stern. Bruce said our fish had picked up two of the other boat's lines.

The yelling became directed at *Misty*, "We're hooked up. We have a double. You handliners think you own the bay. Get the hell out of our way."

Bruce continued to retrieve line, controlling his temper while keeping control of our fish.

As the transoms approached each other, the screaming became louder, more abusive and obscene. Both Bruce and I tried to concentrate on the task at hand while shutting out the obnoxious verbiage. When we had the pot warp almost in, the transoms came together and the first of the *Yellow-Yahoo's* hooks came aboard. Bruce detached it, handed it to the screamie-mimie, and softly said, "Here's your first hook-up." This was followed by the second hook being handed over: "And here's your second screaming hook. Now back that ugly baby-shit-yellow monstrosity away and watch how a real hook-up should be handled!"

Rainbow Boat Follies

Some events that take place in a tuna fishing fleet have nothing to do with tuna fishing. One, in particular, garnished the greatest attention from almost the entire fleet. It happened on a calm morning in early August 1977.

A boat pulled into the fleet about 1000 hrs. and proceeded to anchor in about ninety feet of water, just to the east of the boats arrayed along the drop-off. She drew attention right away because she had a classic old scow shape and looked very unseaworthy; but the real reason for all the attention was her fresh paint job. There had to be at least twenty different colors displayed on her topsides that began and ended in no particular pattern. Most of them were pastel shades and the overall impression was that the paint must have come from cans of left over paint, probably picked out of the P'town dump. Scrawled across her stern, in international orange, was her very appropriate name: *Rainbow*.

The captain and crew of five were all female. The main attraction occurred around 1330 hrs. when the sun had pushed the temperature to "swelter."

The ships company appeared on the foredeck and began, very slowly, to disrobe. Immediately chumming came to a halt on the other boats as binoculars came to attention. Catcalls, whistles, applause and sexual innuendoes began filling the air. This appreciative display grew in intensity until the ships company paired off and turned the fore deck into a "foreplay deck!"

Sunfish Can Be Dangerous

These benign and endangered sea creatures shaped like a huge silver dollar, with tiny fins and a very small tail, have been observed almost clearing the surface of the sea. I have never been privileged to see this personally, but I have read about their exploits, as documented in some learned journals.

A fleet of tuna boats observed an event that took place on the tuna grounds in the mid seventies involving a close encounter between a sunfish and a 32' wooden lapstreak cruiser. The boat was approaching the grounds when it took a hard thumping shock near its port bow. The skipper looked over the side and observed a stunned sunfish as it slid aft into the wake. After anchoring, he noticed the bilge pumps were working and checked below to find a sprung plank about a foot below the water line. Water was pouring in faster than his pumps could handle and the boat was down by the bow.

He put in a call to the CG, who sent a whirly-bird to drop a Handy-Billy pump to the vessel. The added pump enabled the skipper to return safely to his homeport. Bottom line? Any collision at sea could cause a boat to be the bottom line.

Reverend Moon Holds Court

Rev. Sun Myung Moon at age 16 claimed Christ had appeared to him and selected him to rid the world of Satan. He founded the Unification Church in 1954 in his native Korea and by 1974 it had become an international multimillion-dollar religious and business enterprise.

The tuna market attracted his attention and he went to North Carolina and bought a boat manufacturers entire output. These boats joined the fleet at the end of the 1970s. He had also purchased a 42' Pacemaker cruiser, *New Hope,* to oversee the operation.

Each morning his crew, male and female, would appear on the foredeck, all in white, on their knees and bowing toward the bridge. Moon would then climb the ladder and invoke the Lord's blessing on his fleet for a good catch, and then give his instructions to the assemblage on the foredeck.

When he reclined for meditation, the crew would scuttle back to their tasks, leaving Moon to himself.

When one of the boats in his fleet caught a fish, its first obligation was to swing by *New Hope* to receive praise and be blessed by Moon. Of course, the boat's skipper had to bow and show his supplication and love for the "Big Boss" before heading for harbor to sell the tuna and increase Moon's warchest.

Conversation With A Mooney

One tuna trip, I was anchored close to a Moonie boat and curiosity took over; the skipper was very tall and he had Arian features with a very blond head of hair. My curiosity was peaked because the other skippers I had seen had oriental features.

Misty was positioned almost dead ahead of the Moonie boat and by letting out more anchor rode we settled within easy talking distance.

"Good morning, due you speak English?" The blond answered, "Yes I do."

"I'm very puzzled. Where are you from and would you mind me asking you some questions?"

"I'm from Norway and no, I don't mind."

"Do you have a family?" "Yes, a wife and two children, a boy and a girl."

"My family is the same. You're on a Moonie boat, are you a member of the Unification Church?" " Yes I am and I'm fishing for the Reverend Moon."

"I've heard that all the income from fish caught by his boats goes entirely to his Church. Does this mean you're not compensated for your hard work?" "We are supplied with a boat, fuel, tackle and chum; we need nothing more."

"The Captains of the local vessels are trying to make a living fishing for tuna. We have expenses and bills to pay. How do you make a living with no compensation?" " I have no need for money because I have no debts."

"With no income, how do you feed, house and educate your family?" " The Reverend Moon gives us shelter, food and supplies us with all we need. He will educate my children, so we neither ask nor wish for anything more."

I had the mate haul in the anchor rode to return to our original position. As he did this, I asked one more question to which I received no answer: "You seem to have everything you want or need except for one valuable commodity — Does Moon also supply you with FREEDOM?"

Bruce Takes A Hook And A Fish

"Here he comes again. It looks as if he knows which chum chunks have the hooks and those that don't. This is the second time he has eaten his way up our slick all the way to-the transom!" I could tell Bruce was not only agitated, but was figuring out how to get this fish to take a hook.

I watched the bluefin turn 180° and go down our slick about four boat-lengths beyond *Misty's* transom, where he again did a 180° and started to eat his way back up the slick. I climbed down from the bridge and took over the chumming duties.Bruce armed the cockpit harpoon and then snapped a safety line and tuna ball to the harpoon running line.

I returned to the bridge so I could report the fish's progress. "He has about 30' to go and he's coming toward the starboard quarter."

"I see him — I'm ready for that sneaky bastard now." Bruce raised the harpoon, aimed the dart just aft of the starboard quarter and watched the fish eating his way toward the dart. The tuna made eye contact with Bruce, took a 90° left turn and exploded into action across the transom. As the fish made his move, Bruce lunged toward the port quarter, heaved the harpoon at his nemesis and almost went overboard from his own momentum.

The safety line payed out over the stern and Bruce got a hand on it as he exclaimed: "I stuck that son-of-a-bitch. I hope I button-holed him good!" As Bruce said that, I pulled the quick release and leaped into the cockpit to clear the five other lines, two at a time. I picked up the fifth line, and felt a fish mirroring the movements of the tuna that Bruce was holding. "Your fish snagged the last line before I could clear it. When you pick up line on the fish, I'll coil the other line in its carton until we get that hook aboard so I can free it."

Bruce had most of the pot-warp aboard when he saw the hook, from the snagged line, dangling from a tangled, knotty mess of leader, just above the Sampson cord. The fish was only 150' from the transom and swimming near the surface. "When you get the hook aboard, I'll cut the hook from the leader with the wire cutters, so it won't be a danger if the fish takes off." (This was 1977 and handline leaders were seven-strand cable.)

Bruce pulled the pot-warp in, plus 10' of the Sampson cord and held on while I struggled with the rusty crimping tool. I was able to cut five of the seven strands, when the fish decided to depart and pulled Bruce toward the transom. The slick Sampson cord began slipping through his hands. "Let go, let the fish take line!" I yelled as I watched the hook swing into Bruce's thigh, pinning him hard into the port quarter. There were two barely audible pings as the remaining two strands parted.

He took a bend over the transom with his left hand, held the fish, and with his right hand he reached down to the hook and yanked it out of his flesh. He began hauling the boat to the fish hand over hand with authority! "You hurt me, you bastard, now I'm going to hurt you."

I ducked into the cabin, grabbed a towel to use as a pressure bandage around his thigh. By the time I emerged, Bruce had all the Sampson cord aboard and the fish was only a boat length behind, still towing *Misty* strongly.

I wrapped his right thigh and cinched a half hitch as tight as I could around his now red-soaked right pant leg, and then rearmed the cockpit harpoon. Bruce handed me the leader, snatched the harpoon and said: "Get him a little closer and he's a goner."

When we had the fish bled and were underway to Green Harbor, I told Bruce he probably needed some stitches and had better get a tetanus shot. "I'll clean the boat, take care of the fish and get everything ready for tomorrow's trip."

The next morning, Bruce limped down the ramp and told me his leg was OK, and that he was ready for the next one.

It was more than a week later before I found out that he hadn't even gone to a doctor!

The Quick Pick

This last snippet is a real tuna-snippet. *Misty* was tied along side a P'town dragger (*Liberty Belle*) anchored on the SW corner of Stellwagen Bank. They were already tuna fishing. The mate and I asked to purchase a tote of fresh caught chum. Anxious to get started, I checked the time as a deck winch was lowering the tote to the mate. Just then one of the crew aboard the dragger announced they had a hook-up. The winch operator released the clutch, tipped over the tote, dumping the chum on the mate, and hurried to uncleat our lines.

I swung *Misty* around the stern of the dragger to watch the proceedings. The fish was already along side, splashing on the surface. A weighted tail-rope was lowered to the fish and very quickly cinched tight around the tail. As the fish was hauled from the water, tail first, the Captain appeared from the cabin with a double-barreled shotgun and expertly emptied both barrels into the tuna's head.

The very dead fish was winched over the gunn'el and as it was being lowered into the hull I again checked my watch: The total elapsed time from the hook-up till tuna down into the hull: four and one half minutes.

Chapter 22

The Pre-Cut Chum & The Rubber Gloves

It was one of those days when you know, deep down, that you should have taken it off. Some sixth sense tells you that you will not hook up. You try to deny the feeling; you try to work through it, much like a basketball player does when he doesn't have the hot hand. When you come down with "Tuna-Fever," all sensibility seems to leave your mind and you have to go out every day. You must deny that sixth sense. If you want to catch bluefin tuna, you have to put in your time and pay your dues.

It was early on a Sunday morning in July. *Misty* was on her way to Stellwagen Bank. The usual banter between captain and mate was missing from what little conversation there was. We hadn't had a hook-up for over a week. As barren days continue to pile up, the need for talk diminishes and the crew goes through the day acting much like a silent automatic baiting machine. Talk was confined to what was necessary for anchoring and getting set up for the day's fishing.

It was a little after 0600 when Bo, the mate, put the baits in the water and began chumming. For the next four hours no words were spoken as each of us went about our shared duties.

"Hey Cap, get a load of this guy coming into the fleet," broke the silence. I looked up from the cutting board and watched a new sixteen foot center-console drop its anchor and settle back to a position about a hundred feet off our starboard beam.

The two people on board, (I assumed they were father and son) were dressed in white and looked as if they would have been more comfortable aboard a ketch or schooner with all the amenities, like hot and cold running water, icemaker to be used when one is indulging himself at the bar, galley complete with oven and microwave, and of course, a laundry to keep those starched whites both starched and white.

I mentioned this to Bo. He smiled and replied, "If they hook-up, they are in deep shit. A hook-up would probably ruin their day, not to mention taking the starch out of them and their dress whites."

While Bo kept the slick going, I climbed to the bridge to get a better look. As far as I could tell, they had only two handlines; complete with what looked like brand new baskets and tuna balls. There was no evidence of the usual chum cooler or fish boxes to hold flats of chum. (Most handliners have six or eight handlines and will use as many as six flats of chum per day.) The only other container, visible aboard the vessel was a pure white five-gallon bucket with a tight fitting cover.

I watched as the gentleman opened the access hatch in the console and withdrew a small beverage cooler, about the size of a six-pack. He zipped it open, reached inside and extracted a whole mackerel. After putting the hook carefully through its back, he nonchalantly dropped it over the side. He didn't measure up the running line for a place to attach a balloon (necessary to keep the bait at a predetermined depth). He evidently had nothing aboard to use as floats for this purpose.

The boy, whom I judged to be twelve or thirteen years of age, was very attentive as the man went through this routine. He seemed to be completely engrossed in learning the "proper" method to entice a giant.

I descended the ladder and smiled at Bo, "Keep chumming, but also keep your eyes on this guy. If he has any chum aboard it has to be in that five-gallon bucket, and that's all." Bo grinned and replied, "At least he's broken the monotony. He obviously has no tuna smarts, and I'll bet this is his first trip to the grounds. But I will keep my eye on him. After all, it might just have some entertainment value."

Almost on cue, the man moved center stage and began a silent pantomime. First he drew a pair of rubber gloves from his shirt pocket and very carefully inserted his hands; next he removed the top from the bucket, picked out two pieces of pre-cut chum and tossed one at each of his lines. He then replaced the lid, rinsed his gloved hands over the side, proceeded to remove the gloves, shook them dry, folded them carefully and placed them back in his pocket.

"Cap, Do you believe this guy? I'll bet a day's pay even his tee shirt is starched."

Five minutes passed and our neighbor looked at his watch, then repeated the procedure down to the last detail. Bo stretched his arms up with his palms extended to the sky, and taking on the look of a bishop ready to perform the annual blessing of the fleet, he bowed his head and gave a blessing to our neighbor for safe passage to his homeport. When Bo finished his performance, I raised my eyes to the sky, made the sign of the cross and in my most soulful voice intoned, "If they hook-up it will always be known as the *Immaculate Connection*!"

For the next two hours, while Bo and I chummed heavily, our "sanitary" friend never varied his routine: Every five minutes: the gloves, the bucket, two pieces of chum tossed over the side, one at each of his handlines.

By noon we were almost out of chum, the temperature was nearing ninety and what little breeze there had been was down to zero. My premonition that we would not hook-up was sadly becoming a reality. So far the only good result of the day was that our neighbor to the north had provided a diversion from the barren period *Misty* and her crew were experiencing. Unknowingly, he had provided entertainment that actually had Bo and me talking to each other again.

Bo dumped the remaining herring chunks and the last quart of chum soup overboard and while he and I were cleaning up the cockpit mess, I suggested we go to Race Point to do some bluefish fishing. We both could use a change of scenery and a much needed attitude adjustment. Bo agreed.

After a quick washdown, we hauled anchor and I swung the bow toward our "Mr. Clean." As we idled past him, Bo cupped his hands like a megaphone and shouted, "We're out of chum and on our way to Green Harbor. We wish you all the best of luck." The man waved and with a bit of surprise in his voice, replied, "Why, thank you, thank you very much."

Around 1530, having been rejuvenated by the much-needed therapy of the light tackle blues, we pulled up to the fuel dock in Green Harbor. We had no tuna to talk about for the eighth day in a row, but on this trip we had a tale to tell that was sure to bring out the smiles and chuckles of the local wharf-rail leaners. As we fueled up, I began to relate our now much-enhanced tale of the "Sanitary Bumpkin" and his attentive son.

This story, as with all fish tails, got more exaggerated with each telling. Bo became the straight man, asking the perfect questions and adding just the right follow up. I was half way through the third re-telling when Bo interrupted with a hand on my arm. "Cap, here he comes now and look at the list on his boat."

I looked down the harbor at the center console making its way very slowly toward the fuel dock. The list had to be at least ten degrees to port. I told Bo I hoped there was nothing seriously wrong and to stand by in case we could do anything to help. I felt a sudden pang of remorse about the way we had been talking about the father and son.

As he approached the fuel dock, the reason for the list became painfully evident. Lashed to the port side was a giant bluefin that we estimated to weigh at least 850 pounds. We were so taken aback that neither Bo nor I went to assist in tying him up. We both just stood in *Misty's* cockpit, staring at the fish with what had to be the ultimate stupid expressions of disbelief.

I finally glanced up from the fish and my eyes met those of the sanitary skipper. He smiled broadly, waved his right hand and said, "Thank you, thank you very much".

I swallowed hard, swung my leg over the gunwale and walked toward him with my hand extended. I smiled wanly and with as much sincerity as I could muster, said only, "Congratulations, nice fish." He pumped my hand vigorously and for the third time that day he said, "Thank you, thank you very much."

I was beginning to think his vocabulary was limited to just that phrase when he continued, "This is only my second fish. My boy and I caught our first fish just last Sunday. You see, my job ties me up from Monday through Saturday. I can only get free to fish on Sundays. Today was only our second trip to the Bank for tuna." I extracted my hand from his grip, spun on my heel and strode stiffly back to *Misty*.

Bo looked at my flushed face and said only, "Ain't that a bitch." Taking note of my quizzical expression he added, "OK, I know, you want me to bring a six-pack cooler full of frozen mackerel, a white bucket, with a cover, filled with precut chum, and a pair of rubber gloves for tomorrow's trip, right? I'll bring all those things under one condition; you have to wear starched whites!"

Chapter 23

The Mate Saves The Day

It was just plain hot; one of those days when everything sticks to you and the slightest exertion makes you break out in a sweat that pours from your pores like the ebb tide from the Merrimack River. The breeze was nonexistent and the sea was as flat as the flight deck of the Yorktown.

Ray and I had been taking turns at the chumming since 0700, and as far as we knew, there had been no hook-ups on the SW corner of Stellwagen Bank since we had anchored. It was now afternoon, and the charter-crew had long since decided they had picked the wrong day. All three of them were in various stages of disarray, depending on the degree of their disrobing.

Ray was "chopping and plopping" on automatic pilot, in low gear. I was–just–day–dream–ing. It was another typically exciting day of tuna-wishing! I began to wonder how many of these fishermen would still be here, enduring this heat, if it weren't for the money these creatures were bringing on the Japanese market.

My attention began to wander and I began to think of other times; when tuna fishing used to be fun. In the '60s and early '70s, we fished for "giants" only for the challenge they brought. More than likely, when the leader was in hand, they were cut free, and with a quick salute from the crew and a sudden splash from the fish, the memory of the fight was etched forever in our minds.

"Hey Cap?" Ray's voice penetrated my thoughts. "Take a look at the boat to our north'ard." I glanced off our starboard beam, and had to smile. The *First Time* had three crewmembers aboard when they arrived. Now, one was asleep, sprawled out on the foredeck; one was swimming back and forth, close to the port side, with a safety line tied around one wrist; and the other one, the captain, was in the helm chair with his head back, snoring and trying to sunburn his nostrils. The captain's elbow was resting on the railing and in his hand was a delicately balanced half-full Martini glass with the obligatory olive on the bottom.

"All three of them really look ready for a hook-up. I don't think they've dropped a piece of chum in the water for at least two hours."

"It's OK. The guy in the water can wrestle with the fish until the other two wake up." As Ray said this, one of their balloon-floats went under and there was the muffled sound of it imploding. I yelled, to the guy who was still swimming, that I thought they were hooked-up. He came out of the water like a breaching whale.

Within a few seconds all three were shouting commands at each other and, as a result, nothing was being accomplished. I'll give the captain credit, though; he awoke and finished the Martini, without spilling a drop. As Ray often says, "First things first."

In the ensuing two or three minutes, the crew managed not to set the hook, start the engine, drop the anchor ball, clear the other three lines, or clear the cockpit of the chum bucket and cutting board. They did manage to spill the chum all over the fighting chair, knock the cutting board overboard, and put the reel that had the fish into free spool!

By this time we noticed, the other three rods were throbbing and *First Time's* anchor ball was bobbing. Ray gave me his look of disgust, "Looks like the fish has taken a turn around their anchor-line, after tangling up all three of their free lines." I answered with, "Let's get our gear out of the water. There's no telling which way that fish is going to go next."

By now our charter crew was awake and they all turned-to, to help clear our lines and square away the cockpit. I was about to pull the quick release on our own anchor ball, when it began to bob. Ray said not to pull the release, and we watched as the two anchor balls moved toward each other. Ray looked at me and, with his usual dry humor, said, "I guess one turn around an anchor line deserves another."

The two boats wound up gunnel-to-gunnel, with the other captain begging Ray to help him catch his fish. Ray looked at the total disaster in the cockpit and then asked if was all right with me if he assisted. I said he may as well, and mumbled something about it being impossible for anybody else to hook-up, because no one else in the fleet was using a swimmer as chum. I wished them good luck, as Ray stepped aboard *First Time.*

Grabbing the rod with the bird's nest, Ray told the "swimmer" to cut one of the other lines and strip that spool down half-way. Then, with the captain and "comatose" each carrying a rod, he proceeded to the bow to unwrap *First Time's* anchor ball.

I noticed that Ray didn't set the hook with the bird's-nest rod he was carrying. I knew he wasn't about to induce any more activity from the fish, until he was ready.

I went to *Misty's* bow and unwrapped our own anchor ball. When *First Time* was free, Ray and his entourage returned to the cockpit, which was now laced with some 700 yards of #130 Dacron that the swimmer had stripped from his rod.

"If you want this fish, you've got to listen to me and react to my requests without question or hesitation. The first thing is to put those rods in their rod-holders and clean up all this #%^$@, so we have a safe area in which to work!" As Ray said this, he glanced over and winked at me. I nodded my head and smiled, as much with pride as with amusement. He had taken complete command of the *First Time,* with that one pronouncement.

When the fish settled into its tow-the-boat mode, Ray had the three members of "his" crew hold the tension on all three lines, while he tied a reverse clinch knot between the remaining line on the stripped rod, and the doubled-over line from the hook-up rod. Then he cut the bird's nest loose. Now, with the fish attached to a rod without a bird's nest, Ray was able to quickly reel in enough line to get several turns, beyond the knot, onto the now "clean" spool.

For the next several minutes, all three rods were brought to bear on the quarry; it was a matter of towing the boat to the fish, as he continued to swim slowly to the west. One of the tangled lines worked itself free and "Comatose" cleared it. I heard Ray tell the captain to hold on, as he gave the prey three quick jabs to make sure the hook was set, and to keep the fish working hard.

At this point in the battle, the captain's rod began to vibrate with the telltale signs of the fish having become tail-wrapped. "Our chances just improved by 50%!" exclaimed Ray as he and the captain began to gain line at a steady pace. "Do you have a cockpit harpoon onboard?" The captain answered affirmatively and told "Swimmer" to go below and get it set up.

"Swimmer" emerged from the cabin carrying a 14-foot throwing harpoon and a tangled mass of line that looked like a giant replica of the previous bird's nest. Ray refrained from any expletives and requested, very firmly, that "Swimmer" take over his rod and JUST HOLD ON!

After 15 minutes of untwisting, untangling, and under-his-breath-muttering, a red-faced Ray had the line straightened out. He took the rod from "Swimmer," told him to coil the line, set-up the harpoon, and cleat off the other end of the coil. Then, he and the captain resumed gaining line.

When the fish was in sight, Ray told "Swimmer" to stand by to stick the fish, on his command. He said this somewhat apprehensively, because in the process of getting ready, "Swimmer" had almost decapitated the captain and run "Comatose" through.

He was poised, at the ready, when the two anglers brought the fish alongside. Just as Ray was about to give the command, the dart fell free of the shank! Ray murmured something under his breath, and then exploded with, "I don't believe it! How do you guys ever hope to catch a fish, when everything you do is so completely dysfunctional? Here, hold this rod and keep the fish alongside, while I try to exercise some damage control." In short order, Ray reset the dart, recoiled the line, checked to make sure it was secured to the cleat, and having decided that no one else aboard could hit the water if they threw at the ocean, drove the dart into the fish, just behind the gill plate.

"Where's the tail rope, Cap?" The captain shrugged his shoulders and shook his head. "I knew it! I knew it!" Ray's face reddened and once again he took complete command, after screaming off his frustration. "Take this line and hold this fish close while I put one together!"

After the fish was tail-roped and bled, Ray, noticing that *Misty* had remained close by during the whole episode, proceeded to the foredeck and took a well deserved bow, as the charter crew and I applauded. "Hey, Cap. Get me the hell off this boat! It may be their 'first time,' but it was almost my last!"

Three hours later, back in Green Harbor, after saying goodbye to the charter crew and preparing *Misty* for the next day's trip, the captain of the *First Time* staggered down the pier, Martini glass in hand, and thanked Ray, profusely. After they shook hands, the captain emptied his glass, stuck a crisp new $100 bill in Ray's shirt pocket and then spun on his heels, almost falling off the finger pier.

Watching the captain lurching up the ramp, Ray looked at his new "Ben Franklin," smiled and said, "With what I went through today, I'm going to consider this hazardous-duty pay"!

Capt. Jarvis' personal best

Species	Weight	Year
Cod	72 lb.	1985
Haddock	12 lb.	1974
Pollock	39 lb.	1979
Wolffish	37 lb.	1990
Goosefish	28 lb.	1987
Winter flounder	6 lb., 8 oz.	1940
Summer flounder	4 lb., 12 oz.	1995
Halibut	118 lb.	1976
Tautog	7 lb., 4 oz.	1964
Scup	2 lb.	1997
Black sea bass	3 lb., 4 oz.	1959
Weakfish	4 lb.	1935
Atlantic mackerel	2 lb.	Several years
Striped bass	54 lb.	1985
Bluefish	22 lb., 8 oz.	1972
Bluefin tuna	1,000 lb.	1978
Mutton snapper	2 lb.	2004
Gag grouper	4 lb., 4 oz.	2004

The 54 lb. striped bass and the 72 lb. cod were caught on the same trip southeast of Nantucket Island, Mass. Those two fish were only a small part of a 450 lb. striper catch and over 1,800 lbs. of cod taken aboard Capt. Ronnie Braun's, *Peggy B.* I lost the "pool" that day when Ronnie boarded a cod that weighed 74 lbs!

For the story about the 1,000 lb. bluefin tuna and the $20 wager; check out p. 184, Chapter 21 - *Half A Ton And A $20 Bill.*

Glossary

Bite -Term used when fish are eating actively.

Bimini Twist - Best knot to form double line with bitter end of tuna line.

Breaker string - Small loop of light line secured to handline and attached to cleat to "snap" and set hook when tuna bites.

Bucket - Alternate name for crow's nest lookout

Buttonhole - Harpoon dart through fish and out the far side

Charter Boat - Vessel for hire. (usually 6 persons max.)

Chop and plop - Cutting and broadcasting chum pieces to attract fish

Chum slick - Oily spread from chum to attract fish.

Chum soup - A strong liquid chum made with ground-up baitfish, olive or cod liver oil, and seawater.

Cockpit harpoon - Six or eight foot harpoon for use in cockpit area.

Combo-Charter - Full day charter having two targets, i.e. - tuna & striped bass fishing.

Crow's nest - Platform atop a mast used to sight tuna and for maneuvering vessel.

Dart - The business end of a harpoon. The toggled arrow inserted on the shaft of a harpoon.

Double line - Doubling end of line by tying end to running line to increase strength.

E.T.A. - Estimated time of arrival.

F.A.C. - Flat-Ass-Calm

Flake - A method of laying line in a back-and-forth manner, in a fish-box, to allow for smooth, tangle-free deployment of the anchor rode.

Flying gaff - Gaff with detachable hook tied to safety line.

Gangion - Stand-off line with hook - attached to main line.

Handline - Type of gear and method of fishing using only line, leader and hook.

Head Boat - (see: Party Boat.)

Highliner - Fisherman who consistently has top catches.

I.G.F.A. - International Game Fish Association

Imprinting - Impress a memory migration pattern on a new fish spawn.

Meat fishing - Term used by fishermen when fishing to make money.

Party Boat - A large vessel that takes large groups of individuals out fishing.

Pot warp - The main line of a tuna basket.

Pulpit - A structure mounted forward of bow used as a stand for harpooner.

Quick release - Device to detach from anchor ball immediately after hook-up.

Rode - Line used for anchoring.

Safety line - A 300' line of pot warp with tuna ball and swordfish clip on the ends.

Sampson cord - Strong light line used for handlining, harpooning, quick release system, etc.

Six Pack - (see: Charter Boat)

Stand - Platform for harpooner at forward end of pulpit.

Stick - Alternate name for harpoon.

Swordfish clip - Device used to quickly attach a line to the middle or loop of another line.

Tail rope - Line with eye to form loop to secure tuna by the tail.

Trolling - Tuna fishing with lures (artificial or real baits) towed behind vessel.

Tuna ball - Heavy-duty float used as a fender, a marker for anchor line, a float for handline, etc..

Tuna Mast - Aluminum mast secured to cockpit sole used to sight tuna from crow's nest.

Tuna tower - Structure above the boat's bridge used for sighting tuna and maneuvering vessel.

Walking fish - Snubbing fish and steering through fleet to open water.

Wiring - Bringing fish to boat, hand over hand, by grasping leader.